G000082468

THE
TEXAS
SPIRIT

David M. Smith

Halcyon Press, LLC..
Post Office Box 260
Pearland, Texas 77588
281-992-3131 281-482-5390 Fax
www.totalrecallpress.com

ISBN: 978-1-59095-168-2
UPC: 6-43977-41689-6
Library of Congress Control Number: 2013954939

Printed in the United States of America with simultaneous
printings in Australia, Canada, and United Kingdom.
FIRST EDITION
1 2 3 4 5 6 7 8 9 10

Dedicated To

The Working Texans of Galena Park

Chemical Exchange Industries, Inc.

Texmark Chemicals, Inc.

The Hope and Healing Institute (HHI)

Author Bio

David M. Smith is founder and owner of Chemical Exchange, Inc. and Texmark Chemicals of Galena Park Texas. He was born and raised in El Paso, Texas. He moved to San Antonio during the Korean War. David attended the University of Texas at Austin. Something of a "prodigal son," he moved east to Houston, where he vocationally established himself in the petrochemical industry. As David puts it, "while Petro Chemicals are my primary occupational vocation, bells are the joy of my life."

About The Book

In <u>The Texas Spirit</u> David M. Smith has written a series of spirited and insightful essays about the chemical industry, events and personalities in his life, and his views on trends in the national economy and other aspects of American life that concern him. The zesty style, folksy humor, and unabashed candor combine in this admirable example of the "Texas Spirit."

Table of Contents

INTRODUCTION

Jogging Into The 21st Century

Hi! My name's David Smith. I'm one of over 200 David Smiths in the Greater Houston phone book, 8,000 in Texas, and over 32,000 in the United States.

Since 1973 my wife Charis and I have lived near Rice University. Chief among what I call "spillover benefits" from living across from Rice is the jogging path around its campus that is just a tad short of three miles. We also enjoy events at Shepherd School of Music.

I suit up before dawn most mornings, cross Rice Boulevard and jog around that path. For me, jogging is less than a flat out run but more than a shuffle. A jock I am not and never was, though for over 50 years in the chemical business and most of the 50 years that I've been married, I've jogged around that fine gravel walkway, dropping to only two miles when we sack in. A time or two, I've run what I call my Galena Park Marathon, which is 15.3 miles by way of Ben Milam Square at 1500 Texas Avenue.

You cannot deny your own experience, and mine has been that jogging is the best investment in good health a person can make. The cost is a pair of running shoes, a gym suit, and an hour before work every day.

The result? I feel fine most days.

More important, I rarely have colds or flu, but when I do, they last but for a day. As a little boy growing up in Far West Texas (El Paso), my dad used to have lots of colds and would take dreadful stuff called Citrocarbonate, which tended to spoil his disposition. Pollen in early spring or summer gives our family more irritation than colds or flu.

You may be saying to yourself, "This guy has his sellin' shoes on." Not really, but I'll tell you jogging is high on my short list of priorities.

I have never taken a flu shot and I've <u>rarely</u> been in the hospital, except as a teenager and another time in college when I was bitten by a copperhead and treated with horse serum, to which I reacted violently. A week after the copperhead bite I went down for a count of five. Thankfully I survived.

I wax eloquent on the merits of jogging but I'll lay off, except to say getting a five or seven days a week workout throughout life, with strain on your heart and lungs, will add at least 10-15 years to <u>your</u> life.

So I pack my shorts and Adidas when I travel which has led me into all kinds of adventures. Sometimes at moderate risk I've jogged in major towns like Amarillo in the Texas Panhandle, as far south as Brownsville, and also in East Texas.

Once when I was in Romania, during the days of Dictator Nicolae Ceaușescu, I got to "visit" with some of the local folks, which was amazing since we were only able to communicate with eyes, hands, grunts and smiles, essentially all "nonverbal communication."

Yes, I believe in non-verbal communication.

My resolution on daily jogging goes back to the 1960s

when I met an old gentleman at the YWCA Cafeteria, Mr. W.E. Thompson who was then over 80. Today we might call him a coot. He had religiously kept up his exercise program that began when he and his wife Miss Betty were members of St. Luke's United Methodist Church.

His stated goal in connection with daily exercise was to live to be 100 years old.

One time at the YMCA Cafeteria I asked Mr. Thompson, "How did you get into this habit of daily exercise?" He responded, "Davee" (that's what he called me) "as a young man I boxed, wrestled, as well as played with the Indian Clubs, did gymnastics and worked out on the machines at the YMCA."

When I asked him what he was doing at the time we talked, he replied, "Oh Davee I walk. I walk a lot, all over downtown Houston, three to five miles every day."

Mr. Thompson went on to say that a few years back, before he sold his car, he and his wife "Miss Betty" continued to exercise so that they might live to be a hundred years old. I'm happy to report that he reached his goal.

He made it to 100 years plus a little over a month extra, and "Miss Betty" made it to 98.

What a role model Mr. and Mrs. Thompson provided Charis and me.

A few years back when Charis and I were on vacation with lifetime friends the Langfords, Don and I made a formal pact, really a contract, duly signed, witnessed, and attested by Don's wife that, subject to continued health permitting, and the Lord willing, we too would aim to live to be 100 years old!

Articles today inform us that the ranks of "centurions" are growing in this great nation of ours. A recent "*National Geographic*" has an infant on its cover with the note, "This baby will live to be 120 years old!"

"Aim at nothing and you'll always hit it" is one of my aphorisms at Texmark. Well, Don and I not only aim to make it to a hundred; we hope to make it together, with our wives, and do it as well as the Thompsons.

TEXAS, TEXANS, TEXIANA

1. Texas Citizenship

A drink from a firehose

If Texas is a whole other country, and it is, and if being a Texan means anything, and it does, we do well to consider the sources and dimensions of our unique Texas citizenship.

I was born and raised in El Paso, and except for the two years in the United States Army, I never spent more than two weeks outside Texas. Correction! I worked the better part of a year in Albuquerque, NM, for their Chamber of Commerce but that area was once a part of Texas.

Provincial?   Texas pride?   Maybe some of both.

In my second semester as a sophomore at E.P.H.S. I was working construction on the Student Union at the College of Mines. The school officially opened on September 23, 1914, as The Texas State School of Mines and Metallurgy with 27 students in buildings at Fort Bliss. In 1919 the school's name was changed to the University of Texas Department of Mines and Metallurgy, and in 1920 to the Texas College of Mines and Metallurgy (TCM). The school's name changed again in 1949 to Texas Western

College of the University of Texas (TWC). Finally in 1967 the school's name changed for the last time to the University of Texas at El Paso (UTEP).

When I went off to college it was a 600 mile drive to The University, though today we have to add "of Texas at Austin." Never did I suppose that the ding-a-ling college in our backyard at El Paso, Texas College of Mines and Metallurgy, would one day become the, yes, the University of Texas at El Paso, or UTEP. Say it more than once and it sounds like an Indian war whoop, doesn't it?

U-T-E-P, U-T-E-P, U-T-E-P, U-T-E-P.

When I got to The University at Austin, of course, I took some flack from guys in the fraternity who asked me how I ever got into Texas, being from El Paso? Then I'd hear, "You're not from Texas. You're from New Mexico. Or is it Old Mexico?"

The issue of Texas citizenship comes up in a variety of ways. A basic question is, "What constitutes being an authentic Texan?"

Being born and raised on Texas soil is a sure answer expressed in one of our Texas anthems (should we call them hymns?). I'll say being born here makes you a Texan, especially in our family.

You may think it ridiculous or quaint, but it's true. When my oldest brother Frosty was a medical intern in Boston Children's Hospital, his wife Betty was expecting. Dad, who by then had moved us from El Paso to San Antonio, shipped Frosty Jr. a cigar box of San Antonio dirt to smuggle into the delivery room at Boston Children's

Hospital so Forrest Moseley Smith, III, his grandson, could with certainty claim to have been "born on Texas soil." Today he's a really fine, superb even, real estate attorney here in Houston with a son Forrest Moseley Smith IV, who will in all likelihood will have a son. Cinco? Perhaps.

Like the *Star Spangled Banner* in which "free" is the highest of the high notes, so also is "soil" in the anthem, *The Eyes of Texas*.

True Texans know the songs, but we seldom sing 'em as hymns except on Texas Independence Day (March 2nd), or San Jacinto Day, which is April 29th. These are still holidays for orthodox Texans, and including Ben Franklin.

I always heard that if you have a problem hitting the highest of the high notes (like "free" or "soil"), either Jack Daniels or Johnny Walker can help. But that was in boyhood days before AC was perfected when our family would sneak off in late July to Cloudcroft, NM to enjoy air conditioning *naturally* at 9,000 plus feet altitude. (Say it with a lilt. Come on now, "*naturally!*")

Regarding Texas citizenship, one might ask about other ways to attain it like "jus boli," one's right as a direct descendent of a Texas citizen. Or you might ask, "Can a person take some kind of an exam to qualify for *becoming* a Texan or make it as in taking Texas History?"

It used to be that if you went to public schools in Texas, you *had* to take Texas history two or three times, as well as exams that go with it. By Texas law I took Texas history in Dudley grade school, as well as at El Paso High School, and again when I attended The University, yes at Austin).

Even though my wife Charis was working on her master's degree at LSU when she moved here from

Shreveport, she still was required to take <u>Texas History</u> before she could teach in any Texas grade school.

Texas history is a unique and wonderful subject! At Live Oak Ranch, our family place near Bergheim, my oldest brother and I started collecting books with "Texas" in the title. Ask yourself, does any other state have anything like the *Texas Almanac*, encompassing data on all 254 of our counties, some of them bigger than a half dozen eastern United States?

Texas alone has a comprehensive encyclopedia entitled *"The Handbook of Texas,"* which was first published in two volumes by the Texas State Historical Association in 1952. Now it's up of five volumes, with most articles the work of PhD candidates in history at The University of Texas at Austin.

While textbooks and histories of Texas abound, *Lone Star*, by T. R. Fehrenbach who lives in San Antonio, stands in a class by himself. Dr. Fehrenbach holds a PhD in history from Yale and his writing is both prodigious and prolific. Fehrenbach has more love of Texas in his little finger than most Texas legislators have in their whole bodies, and a whole lot more integrity. To hear him talk Texas history is like taking a drink from a fire-hose or it's best just to read his classic, *Lone Star*, so you can enjoy it at your own pace.

At the UT Law School in the '50s there was a professor, Judge Stayton, who authored *Texas Civil Procedure*, a textbook so big that law students like my brother Paul almost needed a hand truck to manage it. Law students used to say, "Taking Procedure from Judge Stayton is like taking the Bible from God."

Something like this might be said of Dr. T. R. Fehrenbach's definitive Texas history set forth in *Lone Star*. Though he never taught professionally, his single volume is comprehensive and must reading for literate Texans.

I have developed a theory on Texas citizenship that I think holds up consistently. It can be tested on most any Texan you care to nominate, heroes such as Houston, Crockett, Travis, Milam, Bowie, the original three hundred, or your favorite living Texas ex-governor. Perhaps you moved here hoping to get away from other impediments.

It boils down to this: An authentic Texan must be flawed or illegitimate in some respect.

Some years ago, I started collecting biographies of Sam Houston. To say that he was a complex character is manifestly correct. It is my estimate that the total universe of Sam Houston biographies is over a hundred volumes of which I might have a third today. In candor, I've not read them all. But I assure you that books about Sam Houston that go down the trail of making him a scout altogether trustworthy, loyal, helpful, friendly, courteous, kind, etc., are into deep fiction.

Back to our overarching question of what makes an authentic Texan, you might ask questions like, "How long do you have to live in Texas before you're naturalized?

When does the claim become valid?

What about one's identity and family?

What proof of character can you hope to show? What about felony offenses, if any? Health?

Any contagious or social diseases?

What occupations or marketable skills should a Texas immigrant bring?"

Stop! Stop! Stop!

Go down your list. Houston lived for years in a drunken stupor with Indians who called him "Big Drunk." Crockett, considered a statesman, was but marginally literate. Travis was a wide-ranging womanizer. A lot of early Texans came here to get away from debts. Most of the people who came to Texas were trying to make a fresh start, and that's why they tacked up signs or painted GTT on their old home places.

> **"Gone To Texas."**

When early Texans got here they found a lot of other GTT folks making fresh starts, too. They got right down to business rather than wasting time checking credentials, credit ratings, pronunciations or family pedigrees. My great-grandfather Samuel Fountain Moseley summarized it well when he settled in Jefferson, Texas, then a port and the third largest "city" of Texas. He said, "Count every man in Texan honest until he proves himself otherwise."

Texas has always been a great business state, and that's a big part of the reason for its greatness; also, the high level of confidence and acceptance are factors in our prosperity. Who cares about how well-connected you are or whether you're descended like Bostonians from Cabots or Lodges? Who cares if you roll your "r's" or not, or hold your fork right, or scratch yourself in public, or pick your nose, or scratch your rear in public places.

In the final analysis, the mark of an authentic Texan and

only dependable criteria for Texas citizenship is this: You must have at least one obvious blemish or defect embarrassing to yourself or others.

Do you qualify? You don't even have to tell us what it is.

We'll take you like you are.

Welcome to Texas!

2. Far West Texas Hindsight

In 1940 Fort Bliss, Texas was something of an afterthought to El Paso, a city of maybe 50,000 folks when I was a boy growing up there. Assuming the frontier closed in 1890, as most historians say, El Paso made the transition from rough, rowdy frontier town to a highly progressive small city easily and quickly. Fort Bliss first was nothing more than a place where for years, we could go watch a polo game of First Cavalry Division soldiers and their horses vs neighbors.

El Paso has always gone its own way from the rest of Texas economically and culturally. I would say that the as an emerging city it was probably most influenced by New Mexico to the North and Old Mexico to the South. An economic element lending strength to El Paso was free trade with Mexico, the "barriers" which were as easy to negotiate as the Rio Grande was easy to broad jump. The structural underpinnings of the Cordova Island experiment *today* might serve as a model for further Mexico – United States border cooperation. Texas might lead the way out of Red Bluff Lake and maybe a half dozen more free trade islands along our thousand miles of the Rio Grande. Surely the United States has a lot to share with Mexico in the area of crime reduction technology.

In my memory, the high quality of life in El Paso was the result of the effective quarantine of vice, tacitly accepted. Across the river in Juarez, there was more than a little prostitution and drug traffic fueled by marijuana, while Juarez was off limits to soldiers at Fort Bliss to the north in New Mexico there was open gambling, especially slot machines which are without question psychologically addictive. I remember vacationing El Paso ladies at Cloudcroft, New Mexico throwing away handfuls of rolled quarters as long as their respectable husbands could or would fund and fuel them. In those days "working women" got limited respect, teachers and nurses excepted.

In the 1940s, officers' wives stationed at Ft. Bliss were quite rank conscious. My mother was a member of the Military Civilian Club, which met regularly at the Women's Club of El Paso, on Mesa Hill. The ladies would get together to push cookies, sip sherry, and socialize with the Army officers' wives, who tended to cluster around the wife of the current Fort Bliss Commanding General.

Though I was not an "Army brat", I grew up with several of them. My first impression of Army life was that it is boring. I remember once driving through Fort Bliss watching two soldiers with nothing better to do than throw rocks and kick tumbleweeds. There were sure plenty of rocks and endless acres of tumbleweeds on the desert, plus sandstorms to make them tumble.

Things changed dramatically Sunday, Dec. 7th, 1941.

I was nine at the time, and our family was at Nannie's house for Sunday dinner when we began hearing newspaper boys on Montana Street hawking the news. "Extra! Extra! Read all about it. Japan bombs Pearl Harbor!"

Reading the headlines, my dad told my brothers and me, "You boys will never forget this day. What has just happened will change all our lives greatly."

Almost immediately El Paso came alive as Fort Bliss surged with soldiers, activity, and growth. Much of what was formerly empty desert became endless rows of well-ordered temporary barracks. On our minds, in the newspapers, and on the radio daily was news of the war for some months mostly bad news.

But we were going to win this thing. We pre-teens became part of the war effort when Dudley Grade School set up a staging area for a paper drive, and then an aluminum drive.. Aluminum was used to make P-38 fighter planes which our boys flew to shoot down Jap Zeros. During the aluminum drive, some of us kids made decisions that weren't ours to make. I for one left maybe one aluminum pot for my mom to cook the family dinner. This was _war_. If as a kid you couldn't buy a War Bond, you could at least put back some of your allowance and buy savings stamps.

During that time my banker Dad was chairman of El Paso County's war bond drives. We kids in Kern Place asked almost every shopkeeper downtown if we could stick up a war bond poster that was taller than most of us. One poster that I distributed showed a resolute farmer wearing overalls in his wheat field with the caption, "Good Earth, Keep it Ours, BUY WAR BONDS." In my archives, I have a personal letter from Secretary of the Treasury Morganthal thanking us Kern Place kids for our part in promoting war bonds. While my Dad was too old for fighting the war, he headed all seven El Paso County war bond drives, each of which well exceeded its assigned goals.

Less successful were our Victory Gardens that were created to answer the question, "If Rio Grande Valley farm boys were off to war, what from our Rio Grande Valley would we eat?" To this day I simply don't believe pictures or statements on seed packages. As a 10-year-old, I read and followed the directions perfectly, planting maybe 15 rows of vegetables. However, I wasn't about to plant anything as bad as spinach since two of my buddies had eaten some and confirmed that it was as bad as its name sounded or as we thought it was. Still, many of us planted Victory Gardens.

My harvest? Two radishes. Not two rows of radishes but two radishes, period. And as expected, they tasted hot and terrible! To this day I confess to a prejudice against vegetables other than beans, corn, carrots and potatoes. I had never seen any of the other vegetables pictured on seed packages, and just to pronounce the names on the packages made them sound pretty awful!

Take rutabaga. Who would want to eat anything as bad-sounding as "root-a-beggar?" In other parts of the world, rutabagas are primarily animal feed, but in El Paso I never saw any cattle eating it. Why, I can't even imagine an armadillo dumb enough to eat root-a-beggar, and that's what he does for a living   roots or begs. I'll pass, thank you.

Or take squash. It just sounds slimy, like if you stepped on it, your feet would go out from under you.

Squash? Sqush! Yuck!

No, thank you.

The worst of all vegetables is one that sounds like the early stages of vomiting, and that's okra. You really should cover your mouth just to say it out loud. Excuse me a moment but... I have to... uh... okra! We're into slimy stuff. Don't tell me it's good for you.

My Victory Garden in the Second World War was a failure and should have been called a Disaster Garden. But it taught me something, probably not what you might at first think. It taught me how <u>not</u> to like vegetables.

3. Cultural Tea-Sip But Closet Aggie

When I was still a little boy growing up in El Paso, I considered being a farmer, though I probably never said as much to my folks or brothers. Our neighbors across the street in Kern Place were the Stahmanns, who had farms down the Rio Grande Valley and up the valley in New Mexico. Mr. Stahmann was an enterprising farmer, eminently successful growing cantaloupes and pioneering pecans. Another role model was a cotton farmer in Anthony whose son Allen Rhodes was a kid buddy of mine. As pre-teens, Allen and I made spending money picking cotton along with Mexican laborers who were probably illegal immigrants, since they were referred to as "wetbacks."

"Horrors, child labor!" someone will say who reads this.

"What's wrong with hard work for pre-teens?" I ask. Allen and I learned how long it took to fill a ten-foot long cotton picker's sack in a hot summer sun (100º F plus). I doubt that Allen and I ever filled one sack between us, since we worked at a leisurely pace earning a dime per pound and learning the basics of personal economics, what I grew to call Economics 101. A fistful of pennies and dimes definitely beats always being empty-handed. More important, Allen and I were prompted to follow other callings in life, besides picking cotton, since we had a baseline with which to compare job opportunities.

Also as a pre-teen, I embarked on my second agricultural misadventure when I decided to grow a "victory garden" during World War II, primarily because it was the patriotic thing to do. With so many farm boys in the service overseas, how on the home front were we to have enough food to feed our families and neighbors? Good question.

Answer: Grow a "victory garden."

With care and attention, I bought several packages of vegetable seeds at Tidwell Feed Company, things I'd never even heard of before, like... (I spell phonetically) – "root-a-begger," "turn-ups," "call-eee-flowerp," "par-snips," and that dreadfully slimy one that sounded like someone in the early stages of "throwing up" and needing to vomit ... "uh,uh, uh,... oak-rah".

Please understand that in West Texas in the late 1940s, one's diet was pretty much centered on corn, beans, chili and cheese, always potatoes, and sometimes peas and carrots. For breakfast there was always oat-meal (easy and cheap to feed three boys).

Thankfully, we always did have plenty to eat.

Now if you want to say we suffered from cultural deprivation, that's another matter. Today my wife will confirm that there are few vegetables I eat without screwing up my face. In Hammond, Louisiana where she grew up, her daddy taught agriculture at Southeast Louisiana College. Talk about cultural shock. I remember the first time she took me to a shrimp boil at Nack-a-tish (I spell phonetically).

Imagine gracious, civilized people pulling apart what we at El Paso had learned in High School Biology were "crustaceans" (translate, shrimp). They threw these crustaceans into pots of scalding water and boiled them alive! Was this a sadistic rite of some sort? Later I learned that Louisiana people with equal fervor eat even smaller crustaceans affectionately dubbed "mud bugs" that are trapped as they climb out of their small mud pyramids. Some smiling, charming Louisiana lady would wander by to inquire, "Care for some more Romma-lod sauce?"

During that summer of 1960 this West Texan almost blew my budding friendship with Charis Jeanne Wedgeworth when we graduated to the mud bugs. I tried to keep a straight face by thinking to myself that if I were in China I might have to eat "delicacies" like fish heads and rice to keep from starving.

This brings up other things from El Paso days for this cultural tea-sip who came close to being an Aggie during the Second World War when I tried growing vegetables in a 1/8 acre Victory Garden, because it was the patriotic thing to do. The caliche soil produced all of two radishes one summer. I might have done better to have planted my Victory Garden in Draino.

Then I decided to try growing chickens, something quite Aggie-like prompted by two older boys in Kern Place who were in the FFA. Translate: high school Future Farmers of America.

My grandparents raised chickens in town for home consumption, and Granddad Heermans had shown me how to gather eggs and build a chicken coop. With enough saved allowance to invest in 50 chicks, I bought ten each of such grand-sounding chicks as Buff Orphingtons, Rhode Island Reds, Yellow Minorcas, and Plymouth Rocks.

I was in the chicken business!

But during the second night of chicken farming, two or three chicks began to droop and by the next morning had died. The same thing happened the next night, and again the night after that. It seemed they got "the Pip," which for me was an explanation that did not explain. Finally, I raised 18 out of the 50 to full size, whereupon I bargained with my mother to transport the grown chickens to Ayoub Poultry Company for contract slaughter.

Try to imagine my mother driving our Studebaker full of chickens with me facing backward, trying to keep the squawking chickens out of the front seat?

We made it to Ayoub Poultry okay, but the financial bottom line of my chicken venture was a loss, though I did get a few bucks positive on my invested allowance.

My next Aggie misadventure happened years later after I'd moved to Houston from San Antonio and had been married a year or so.

One day I noticed a classified ad in the *Houston Post* that brought my Aggie tendencies to the forefront with a vengeance. The ad ran about like this:

SMALL FARM FOR SALE
**Nearby in Liberty County. Grow produce,
with fruit trees, bearing pecan trees,
14 acres with creek along the back side,
Nice frame house. See owner only
Clarence McCutcheon, etc. etc etc.**

"We need to check this out," I told Charis. "Besides, we now have a nest egg we can put into it. This could be the opportunity of a lifetime."

It was love at first sight. Mr. McCutcheon was at work in his fields, every inch an authentic farmer, even to soil under his finger nails. And, he scratched his bottom with aplomb.

Though the house was at the front of the property, there were two parallel rows of huge mature pecan trees extending toward Caroline Creek.

"Just look, Charis," I rhapsodized. "Someday we can build our dream house at the end of that double row of pecan trees."

I was sure of my intention to build a house at the end of the two rows of pecan trees, and was equally sure in my resolution then and there to start growing more pecans, although I was conscious of the fact that Charis was not as enthusiastic about "Aggie-culture" as her liberated husband was.

Within a week, I was on the phone to Billy Stahmann, friend and neighbor from El Paso days then living in Las Cruces, New Mexico. Like I had good sense and had already converted to being a farming Aggie, I got down to business. "Billy, this is Davo. I've just bought a farm near Houston and I'm going to plant our fields in pecans. How soon could you ship me a hundred seedlings or whatever the heck you call baby pecan trees?" Billy heard me out and then shipped me a hundred trees.

Within days I had parked my fragile chemical business to plant fledgling pecan trees, assisted by a Mr. Roundtree in Dayton, an old man who operated a tiny tractor having a "three-point hitch." Now a "three-point hitch," in case you're not an Aggie, is something any authentic farm boy, Aggie or not, knows to be as basic as a hoe (or today, a chain saw).

As an aspiring farmer/Aggie I had bought (not rented), a heavy 30 inch diameter soil bit from an agricultural supply company. I was sure that I would soon be planting pecan trees by the hundreds or even thousands, and have a tractor and three-point hitch of my own to tie on to my huge Auger.

The day came to start planting.

D-Day! Up men, and to your posts! The noise of Mr. Roundtree's backfiring engine was wonderful, like that of men going into battle. The contrast between Mr. Roundtree's tractor and my heavy treehole drill was grand as the bit chewed into tough gumbo topsoil readily.

As I listened to all the tractor noise as he engaged the clutch, I thought for a second that Mr. Roundtree and his tractor would be going up and around for a spin, if the big drill bit should hit a big rock.

Oh, me of little faith! Some three days later, with the holes all dug and the one hundred plus pecan saplings planted, Charis and I might have planned to live happily ever after.

Not quite.

I had sense enough to water my new trees regularly, but within 60 days I noticed some dry ones when I scratched the bark to check for life. I had lost more than a few, indeed half or more during the second year that passed. But again with Mr. Roundtree's help, I ran the play once again with pretty much the same results planting saplings from the Stahmanns' farm. The third year was a repeat performance of years one and two.

"When you need your teeth fixed, go find a dentist," my former roommate and best friend Arnold once told me. So, I made contact with Texas Pecan Growers Association, where I figured I could "find the dentist," so to speak, to address my problem in need of fixing. Aggie pecan growers accepted me as a dues-paying member, no questions asked, for their Pecan Growers Short Course in the fall. I also had to swallow some of my Texas pride, for clearly I was throwing darts at a board in a dark room when it came to growing pecans. I had a problem and I knew enough to acknowledge it, which is the first step.

I arrived mid-morning during the coffee break for the opening session of the Short Course held at Texas A&M College Station. Everyone was wearing a name tag. I decided to list Dayton, Texas instead of Houston as my home town on my name badge. I reasoned it might make things easier, being so obviously a non-authentic Aggie.

A laconic country boy in coveralls ambled up to me and stared at my name badge.

"Dayton, Texas?" he intoned slowly and disbelievingly.

Then with a slow troubled look he inquired, "You can't grow any pecans in Dayton... can you?

There was embarrassed silence.

"Not as far as I'm concerned," I responded. "That's why I've come to this meeting. I need to learn why with three years planting over 100 pecan trees each year just like you're supposed to do, I lose a third of my trees each year."

There was another embarrassed silence.

"Oh," was my new friend's sole response as he walked away.

Soon the articulate instructor reconvened the class and jumped right into his subject, which dealt with promising new *"eastern varieties* of pecans in Texas..." By the end of the hour, the scales had dropped from my eyes when I was given to understand something as obvious and fundamental to Aggies as water not running uphill. The short version is East is East, West is West, and never the twain shall meet when it comes to growing pecans in Texas.

I had been trying to grow western pecan trees from the dry desert area near El Paso in the heaviest rainfall part of the state, east of Houston!

Dumb me. Perhaps I should cut myself some slack and charge this mistake off to the fact that I'm a slow learner.

It was time for an agonizing reappraisal, especially since my third time trying to grow pecan trees was assuredly not the charm. Racing back and forth from Dayton to Houston pushing my emerging chemical business was tough enough. Allowing my latent Aggie instincts open expression was proving even harder.

One day during a visit with my ex-college roommate and...UT Fiji friend, Les Moor, he took on the role of Dutch uncle and said, "Dave, if you're going to live in Dayton, *live* in Dayton. If you're going to live in Houston, *live* in Houston. But *decide!*" I walked around Les's wisdom a time or two or three. Socially we weren't fitting in at Dayton, perhaps because I wasn't a rice farmer. For all I know it might have been because I didn't have dirt under my fingernails like Mr. Roundtree or didn't pick my nose or scratch my rear-end with finesse.

In a last ditch effort to get out of the Aggie closet or at least to make some friends at our Dayton "farm", I told Charis, "Darlin', with some of my acquaintances at the Dayton Barber Shop and some of yours through the Baptist church, let's invite some couples to a supper party at our new frame house. We'll set up card tables and borrow folding chairs. You can fix spaghetti and we'll see who comes. Goodness knows, we have ordinary social instincts."

Invitations were extended early and careful preparations were made for fourteen couples. Card tables, candles, and decorations, plus good weather, were in place when we did indeed find out "who comes."

One couple came out of the fourteen invited.

After supper and pleasantries, the one couple took their leave. Charis might have cried as she looked at the roomful of empty set card tables and candles. Though my feelings were hurt, I faced the fact that I wasn't fitting in. This realization should have dawned on me earlier when I wasn't asked to join the "volunteer" fire department. Either way clearly this tea-sip didn't make the cut as an Aggie.

As I expressed it to Charis, "Darlin' I don't know if we're not good enough or not crummy enough."

As a sop to the suppressed Aggie in me, 15 years later, this tea-sip planted three sapling pecan trees of different varieties across our front lawn in Houston, emphatically eastern, Texas varieties. I'm a slow learner, but hopefully I *do* learn. Today these pecan trees are large and beautiful.

They also bear pecans quite adequately, but unfortunately the squirrels are the sole beneficiary of my three-hour short course at Texas A&M and three years pecan farming in Dayton.

However, my war with the squirrels is another "war story" that will wait for another day.

4. Live Oak Ranch, Bergheim, Texas

After moving from El Paso to San Antonio in the fifties, Dad Smith surprised his family by doing something at variance with two of his banker aphorisms: (1) It's easier to borrow than to pay back, and (2) Don't own anything that eats.

He bought a medium-size ranch north of San Antonio, financed by a loan from an insurance company. Then he put a herd of white-faced Hereford cattle on it and later Texas Longhorns.

Dad named it Live Oak Ranch because he so appreciated the trees on his place. As a boy, Dad had moved from the piney woods of deep East Texas to the stark desert of far West Texas which has no trees, period. He must have felt like he was coming home when he bought the ranch in Comal County with plenty of trees, most of them large handsome Live Oaks. We still have his framed copy of the poem by Joyce Kilmer that starts off, "I think that I shall never see a poem lovely as a tree." Dad wasn't into poetry, but he was sure into trees now with hundreds of Live Oaks he could call his own. He named the place well, even though you can be sure that there are lots of Live Oak Ranches in Texas and elsewhere in the Southwest. The *Handbook of Texas* shows 20 Live Oak Creeks alone. Ranches are sure to be more numerous than creeks.

Dad didn't buy the place solely for its trees, but rather

as a working ranch. He had made lots of cattle loans in his banking career, especially in El Paso at State National Bank. Now he would experience how tough it is to make a profit running cattle under any scenario. To say that one's perspective from the borrower's side of a loan desk is different from the banker's side is an understatement, but Dad had to make that shift when he borrowed to buy our family ranch.

What a happy surprise it was for all of us Smiths, and what a challenge for him. The maintenance under previous ownerships extending back to the days of the Republic had been negligible to minimal. One of the previous owners was a bootlegger whose "process hardware" as we call it in the chemical business, was located in the draw north of the house to keep it out of sight during Prohibition. Some of that junk plus beer bottles and pop cans lying around ankle deep were still around in the late 1950s. Dad didn't hesitate to call on his three boys, now grown and one married, to help clean and shape up our new place, Live Oak Ranch.

An afterthought at closing was something of a joke. Dad bought a little red truck for one dollar that came to be called just that, the Little Red Truck. It was a 1942 Ford pickup with a clutch and a straight stick shift on the floor. It was a sinkhole of maintenance costs but a source of great fun. With Dad driving slowly and us boys in back, we had fun picking up the cans and assorted junk, laughing and acting like little boys again. Each haul was consolidated in a defilade area still referred to as "The Dump."

In the early years, on Dad's orders, it became my fun job to rebuild and repaint the small stake body of the Little

Red Truck. More than once we would see how many Smiths we could get on it and or in it, great for photographs. In Kendall County, Live Oak Ranch was probably the best customer for repairs that Anderson Ford ever had. In terms of repair bills we probably paid for a new pickup three times over, till finally one day the Little Red Truck (like all of us ultimately) was past going. We put it away under the side shed of the hay barn.

As a viable working ranch, Live Oak was managed by our neighbor to the north, Mr. Dierks, who checked the livestock daily. Dad always ran Herefords, a conservative breed and conservative in number; never overgrazing Live Oak as so many ranchers tend to do. These days we grass lease to a man who runs Texas Longhorns. Some would say that longhorns give a more "marbled" kind of beef and that they're smarter than other cattle. It is likely true that longhorns can survive on less water and feed. But those very long corkscrew horns are mighty funny-looking.

Four horses came with the property: Paint, Bateen, Prince, and Blue, but in time the horses became entirely recreational. All ten of Dad's grandkids learned to ride horseback at Live Oak and also got to drive over the place as much as they cared to.

Smith grandkids were usually three years ahead of their peers learning to drive with the Little Red Truck, legally but without a license, only on Life Oak Ranch. Learning to clutch and use the stick shift on the floor was as much fun as horseback riding. With parents' permission, grandkids and many other visitors could drive alone around the two-mile loop east of the house. I remember when my pre-teen son David Jr. qualified to drive alone. He must have made the loop within the ranch fifty times or more in one weekend.

In the spring when bluebonnets are at their height, I head over to San Antonio to attend the annual convention of National Petrochemical and Refiners Association (NPRA). This convention is important to my chemical business, and a Live Oak Ranch barbecue is sometimes part of the fun.

It was just after one of the NPRA parties had ended that it became my sad duty to have to "put down" old Blue, the last of our original four horses that came with the ranch when Dad bought it from Mr. Steeves. Blue was old, very old, and unable to run with the other horses. It was pitiful to see him that day half standing but dragging his hind legs. There was but one thing to do. I went inside and got Mr. Flory's 30-30, came back out and looked at old Blue for the last time. I put a cartridge into the chamber. Then you know what followed.

I phoned Harold Dierks, who came over, and with the help of the Little Red Truck we tied a rope to Blue's hind legs and dragged him to an oak on the hill where Harold noted Blue liked to hang out in previous years. I thought that was a nice touch, kind of like throwing the ashes in the backyard or pasture of someone who's been cremated.

I like to say that Live Oak Ranch is a "nothin' place," i.e., no one has to do nothin' they don't want to do, nothin'! Please understand, however, that this nothin' place don't have nothin' to do with the negative ten letter "r-word" (retirement).

Now I'm not looking for a fight or even an argument with anyone, but for some fundamentalists, this point: Find me one place is all scripture, a reference even, touching on "retirement." How are we going to make our living when pettifogging politicians' Ponzi Scheme centerpiece called Social Security goes broke sooner rather than later?

I think I speak for many Smiths who are opposed to retirement. I'll have more to say about that in "Working Texans of Galena Park." But when we make our bumper stickers at Galena Park, one will say ABOLISH RETIREMENT. I plan to put the first one on the Little Red Truck at Live Oak Ranch, both back and front bumpers.

By the way, there's a new brand of wine out now called, "Red Truck" but our truck at Live Oak Ranch has no connection with it.

Let's get back to the story of how we acquired the Little Red Truck. In the 1970s when the original pickup was finally "put down" or at least retired to the side shed of the hay barn, Dad bought and paid cash for a bright red new pickup from Jennings Ford in Boerne. It then became Little Red Truck II. It, too, had a stick shift with clutch, with the gearshift on the steering wheel. When it was ready to be retired (or put down), I made a career shift at the chemical plant for a tuned up Ford and painted it bright red. It became Little Red Truck III for Live Oak Ranch.

When we're at the ranch we invariably go to the Bergheim Store, formerly Engel's Store in downtown Bergheim, Texas (population 85). The store is three miles west from our front cattle guard and pretty much like Mr. Engel built it over a hundred years ago, when he emigrated from Germany. Stanley Jones, who owns Bergheim Store today, is postmaster and great grandson of the late Andreas Engel.

The write-up in *The Handbook of Texas* on Bergheim

mentions that it once had the largest cedar yard in the State of Texas. There's another interesting bit of history mentioned in the *Texas Almanac*. During the Great Depression, Andreas Engel, a compassionate, frugal German grocer, fought both poverty and unemployment by extending credit to anyone who would go out and chop cedar, then rack it up. Mr. Engel nearly went broke himself, but over a period in the late 1930s he was able to sell his acres of stacked cedar a little at a time in San Antonio, 30 miles to the south.

How I wish there had been more people like Andreas Engel and fewer like FDR and his ilk in the 1930s who saddled us with runaway government that we endure today. Runaway government most definitely must STOP.

It was my pleasure to give a pole-mounted locomotive bell to Mr. Engel's great grandson, Stanley Jones, when he celebrated the hundredth anniversary of Bergheim Store in 2003. The bell stands in tribute to all forebears who came here to live in freedom before or since 1903; i.e., German, Hispanic, whoever and from wherever, if they believe in God and freedom.

Meanwhile back at Live Oak Ranch, there have been good times too numerous to count. Buddy's daughter Alexine and her husband Peter had their wedding reception there, built a house on some carved out acreage, and raised their kids up there. Friends of my brothers at First Presbyterian Church of San Antonio use it and enjoy it, as do our Baptist friends, and others. It's great for barbecues and entertainment generally.

Fourth of July is sometimes something of a homecoming, with our son, Davo, as Resident Director of

Fireworks, at least when he's in Texas. After a hard Fourth at the pool and a day of watermelon, barbecue, Aunt Charis' pies, Aunt Betty's cookies for "snacks" plus unlimited cokes, not all of the now older generation, that's us, are willing to stay awake till 9 p.m. for the fireworks. Oh, we manage provided we can get a nap.

Today those of us over 70 years old are a fraternity I call "Los Viejos."

Like compound interest, the arithmetic of family increase is astounding. Keeping the best of the past yet responding to economic change is challenging. Problems notwithstanding, we work toward optimal employment and stewardship with fellowship in this splendid legacy Dad Smith gave us, which is now emerging into the fifth generation. Soon there will be Little Red Truck IIII; that's right. Maybe I'll live to see Forrest Moseley Smith the Fifth.

My hope and prayer is that not only all living descendants of Dad Smith, but their spouses, in-laws, outlaws, shirt tail relatives, cousins, first, second or removed, plus friends of the above can all enjoy Live Oak Ranch in this 21st century even a fraction of as much as I have. My hope and prayer is that we within the David Smith branch of our extended family will never cut it up just to make chili out of it (Translate: sub-divide it just for short-term quick cash).

Personally, I am committed to this end.

5. Texiana Pearls and Water

By a fortunate set of circumstances in the late 1950s, I was able to purchase an extraordinary collection of Texiana from the estate of William A. Philpott, who for 50 years was Secretary of Texas Bankers Association. Mr. Philpott had been a lifetime friend of my banker dad before the days of television. He collected nearly 2,000 items of early Texas memorabilia, especially letters and documents from the years of the Republic, throughout his travels over Texas. Such items are properly designated Texiana.

Mr. Philpott had talked to several institutions, especially the University of Texas, about selling his collection, but nothing came of it. Because of his friendship with my dad, I was able to visit him in the Mercantile Bank Building in Dallas where he housed his marvelous collection. What an experience it was to hear Mr. Philpott tell stories as he thoughtfully examined his items, each of them a pearl of Texas history.

When he died, the executor of his estate contacted all institutions and persons who had manifested any interest in the Philpott collection. I was flattered when the trustee contacted me, because I sure didn't have the money it would take to buy Mr. Philpott's Texiana Collection.

The collection was not your proverbial "pearl of great price" but rather like many boxes of them, each document a "pearl" with a story to go with it.

Mr. Philpott had expressed two preferences in selling his awesome collection: (1) that it be sold intact, not piecemeal; and (2) that preference be given to a "younger collector" having an interest in Texas history and Texiana. On age I was then in my 30s, and on interest I presumably qualified, having once been awarded the history medal at El Paso High School.

In the 1940s the Texas Legislature required that all students study Texas history in Texas schools and colleges. As mentioned earlier, I had taken something of a triple dose, at Dudley Grade School, at El Paso High School and at The University of Texas. However, I truly enjoyed Texas history. I didn't think of my studies in this subject as doses of medicine to be tolerated but rather as big helpings of Blue Bell Ice Cream to be enjoyed. I love our state as much as any Texan [but today I am as opposed to mandatory Texas history as I would be to a Texas Commissioner of Propaganda or Thought Police, something akin to a Texas NKVD. Horrors! Yes, NKVD (thought police any one?)].

Surely I was no historical heavyweight, but what I lacked in knowledge I made up for in enthusiasm. While I didn't have the funds, neither did the Texas schools or museums at that time. I stayed in touch with the Philpott estate executor for months, and finally I agreed to his price and he agreed to my terms: no down payment, reasonable interest, and monthly installments over ten years while the collection was held in trust.

We had a deal! Meeting my payment obligations was not easy, but at the end of 120 months I took possession of The Philpott Collection of Texiana pearls, as planned and agreed.

The collection included 62 letters or business documents with the signature of Sam Houston, his rubric, and in some cases with his own wax seal affixed. This was the centerpiece. There was an impressive sub-collection of Austin family materials including Stephen Austin's letter to the Gonzales volunteers. Also there were seven items written and signed by semiliterate Davy Crockett and four by William B. Travis.

Altogether there were more than 900 items of historical interest from the early days of the Republic. What a unique pleasure it was to peruse them! This was the high point of my ownership of Texas historical pearls, the few years before Texas' Depression of the '80s when I owned the Philpott Collection free and clear and had full possession.

In the '80s, I found myself in deep trouble financially. Not only was it a bad time for Texas; it was the worst time known by my line of work making and selling specialty petrochemicals. This was further compounded by an explosion at my Baytown plant that was a tragedy literally, legally, and financially.

When I looked at the large debts on my books, I had to face the fact that I had exhausted all sources of money except the Philpott Collection which had appreciated over the years. So to hopefully optimize a sale, I engaged a New York appraiser who ostensibly knew values of rare documents and books. Pursuant to his machinations, the appraiser responded with an esoteric written report and two scenarios. If the collection were sold piecemeal over two or three years, it could be expected to bring $4.3 million.

Wow! That would pay off my entire personal "national

debt!" But my big payment obligations to some 200 creditors, many of whom, though I technically wasn't legally responsible for, wouldn't allow me to wait the two or three years it would take to sell all the individual pieces in the collection.

The appraiser opined that with a well promoted and organized sale, engaging the services of some high profile Texan, the collection could bring on the order of $2.7 million. The name of retired Governor John Connally was mentioned, and I was able to meet him. As he chewed on his cigar and blew smoke, he expressed a willingness to handle the promotion and sale of the collection through his art and antiques firm.

So I "went into my closet," so to speak, to think, to pray, and to consider my options, which were few. To sell the marvelous Philpott Collection at auction would be about as much fun as putting your kids up for adoption. Though not formally pledged, I wasn't being pressured by anyone to sell it at least at that time. I had made slow progress paying my debts from three pages of creditors to less than two pages, having completely paid off many of the smaller ones. I had also undertaken other measures like moving out of our homestead on Rice Boulevard to put it at full risk beyond the Texas homestead exemption. What was the right thing for me to do? I was the one who was responsible for this morass of debt. I was the one who had guaranteed such large notes.

The best course of action seemed to be to have Governor Connally's firm sell my Texiana pearls of great price at auction. I resolved to move forward with the one-time auction, sad though that would be, and signed a formal contract.

The sale was held at the Dallas Hilton in October 1986. Specially qualified persons and institutions had been invited to the see-and-touch sessions the day previous, and a moderate number had responded. Supposedly hundreds of potential buyers from Texas and throughout the country had been invited to the events by ex-Governor Connally and his partners. Pursuant to making a formal commitment to Gov. Connally, I learned that his debt was a multiple of mine. Sale day arrived. There were specific times scheduled for selling the subsets of the collection: Travis, Crockett and ultimately the large Houston collection.

But where was Governor Connally?

As the morning of the second day progressed, I asked, "When is he coming?"

The short answer was slow in coming, "He wasn't." I learned that the governor's commitment was no more substantive than his cigar smoke, at least to me.

The day wore on; the numbers were moderate at best, with the auctioneer trying to build interest and enthusiasm. Prices were disappointing. About 5:30 p.m. we broke for dinner, resuming for a final two-hour evening session that was somewhat better attended.

Then it was over.

The final results were dismal. The auction brought nothing remotely approaching either of the appraisal figures prepared by the Connally men. The higher dollar number would have cleared all my personal debt, the lower figure that would have knocked it down substantially. The gross proceeds were a disappointing $367,000, less than a fifth of Gov. Connally's pessimistic appraisal figure.   Adding insult to injury was the 15 percent commission off the top paid to Governor Connally's outfit.

In fairness I might say that the poor state of Texas' economy MIGHT have been a bigger factor in the punk results than the poor performance of Governor Connally. But he definitely should have been physically present for at least a portion of the auction, if no more than to give a 10-minute pep talk to the attendees.

The good news was that I could go around to my creditors and make appreciable payments, expressing once again my commitment to repay the outstanding principal, albeit with little or no interest. But, with appreciable "cash in my blue jeans," so to speak, I was always welcomed by a creditor. Some parties who had been skeptical expressed renewed confidence in me, especially five Houston banks I owed money to, or had secondary stand-by guarantees to.

A word of encouragement fitly spoken can have remarkable impact to persons in distress. I could name several persons, some but acquaintances, whose good words helped see me through this dark period in my life, especially members of South Main Baptist Church.

Robert Louis Stevenson had an aphorism concerning hope, so dripping with wisdom that it sounds almost scriptural. "It is better to travel hopefully than to arrive."

Though I had yet miles to go to keep my promises, it was a bright experience of hope each time I made even a token payment to one of my creditors. Indeed, I was "traveling hopefully," however long or far it might be to the final outcome.

Addendum: It took me 15 years.

6. Texas Medical Center

Though I've said it before I'll say it again, I don't want to be sick anywhere, but when my time comes to be dreadfully sick, I want to be right here in Houston close to Texas Medical Center, with its 42 institutions and 15 hospitals staffed by multiple tens of thousands of medical professionals. Today with the Internet, there is most probably someone who "knows what page of the book we're on", whatever our malady, pain, or infection.

When I was a kid in El Paso in the '50s, I used to think a person felt better about a medical problem if the doctor could just put a name on it. Sometimes it seemed to me that the doctor was just "throwing darts at a board in a dark room" when he would give an elaborate name for a disease or an explanation that did not explain.

I don't think this sort of thing happens very often these days inside the Texas Medical Center.

I remember when my oldest brother, Dr. Forrest Mosely Smith, Jr., was an aspiring pre-med who later did his residence in pediatrics at Hermann Hospital. I was selling dry ice at the time to M. D. Anderson Hospital, to Hermann Hospital, and to other med center institutions, but especially Baylor Medical School where high-powered research work required near instant freezing of human tissue at sub-zero temperatures on expiration of patients. Morgues are grim places, but I got used to several of them in T.M.C., delivering two inch thick, one foot square solid carbon dioxide slabs, often late at night or by pre-dawn's early light.

Today our home on Rice Boulevard faces Rice Stadium and is a short mile from the Med Center. We've watched it grow from early days when it was referred to as Houston's "second downtown."

Each morning an army of thousands who've invested their lives in healthcare drive in to Texas Medical Center from all directions. You might say most of the Med Center employees have "enlisted in the T.M.C. healthcare army, for a lifetime." In addition to the paid healthcare professionals there are other thousands of volunteers who don't receive a cent for their substantial contributions to our healthcare system.

Last year Dr. Dolph Curb, a lifetime member of the South Main's medical fellowship network passed away at age 103. This highly esteemed gentleman/physician/writer had in effect given three lifetimes of service to and/or within the Texas Medical Center.

It slightly annoys me that Houstonians have so little idea what goes on in my line of work, which is the chemical business. Is my business comparable to what goes on within Texas Medical Center? The short answer is lots. Though I jog by it almost daily, I know that far more is happening than just hospitals making sick people well. We've largely won the battle against heart disease and have made awesome progress against cancer and other diseases, using today's consistently advancing medical technology.

Think for a moment of the men who founded the

institutions of our Texas Medical Center and how mostly individuals paid for the hospitals within its borders out of personal funds. With the exception of Ben Taub Hospital, nearly all of our institutions arose in the private sector and with private, non-government funds. Most of the hospitals were Christian-based when they started, and hopefully some still are. Each institution's history is a remarkable story that moves onward and upward with deliberate speed and sustained progress.

Consider Hermann Hospital. George Hermann was a bachelor Swiss immigrant who had experienced poverty and what it was like to be desperately in need of medical care but be unable to find it. When he became prosperous, he gave both Hermann Park and Hermann Hospital to the citizens of Houston. Hermann was a not-for-profit charity hospital initially when he gifted it to the citizens of Houston. His legacy is the Memorial Hermann Healthcare System, with eight satellite hospitals in the Houston area alone. My view is that George Hermann was truly the "Father Abraham" of Texas Medical Center.

Montrose D. Anderson, like George Hermann, was also a bachelor, exceptionally wealthy and frugal to an extreme. He made a fortune trading in cotton and gave us the international cancer research facility that bears his name, The M.D. Anderson Foundation.

Dr. Denton Cooley and Dr. Michael DeBakey are names familiar to most Houstonians. These men did pioneering work developing technology in fighting heart disease and cancer. Each was a general. "General" Dr. DeBakey's "army" was at Methodist Hospital and "General" Dr. Cooley's Texas Heart Institute "army" was at St. Luke's

Episcopal Hospital. These professional healthcare armies annually perform hundreds even thousands of open heart surgeries, cardiac cauterizations, and heart transplants.

All of us know that we are beginning to win the continuous war against cancer, heart disease, and many other diseases with spectacular victories. The "combat information center" for much of this fight is M. D. Anderson Hospital and Cancer Center, which serves not only Texans but patients from all over the world.

In my younger years whenever a person got news of cancer it was like a death sentence. Implicit in the word "cancer" was little or no hope. When you heard the diagnosis you'd silently say to yourself, "Old Schultz won't be with us much longer." And he wasn't.

Then we started hearing the terms: chemotherapy, radiation treatment and in remission. People began surviving cancer and enjoying added years of life. Thankfully today, 20 years, 50 years, and near normal remaining lifetimes are not unusual, provided the cancer does not "metastasize" and they "got it all." While one in four of us will likely die of cancer, survival rates continue rising. Five-year relative survival rates for men were in the 30% range before 1960; today here in Texas the survival rate pursuant to aggressive treatment is well over five years.

Impressive gains have also been made in reducing the cancer death rate for women, dropping 30% over 50 years. Here I salute the Susan G. Komen Breast Cancer Foundation and its annual "Race for the Cure" for breast cancer, where thousands participate in a walking, wheelchair, and jogging event in Houston. What a wonderful example of dealing with medical challenges in the private/voluntary sector.

With gratitude some thoughtful cancer persons have created the Cancer Survivors Plaza in the Texas Medical Center. It reminds me of one particularly important fact. We Texans, indeed all who have had to deal with the tough, disagreeable aspects of cancer treatment, do well to give thanks for the measurable and growing sophistication of treatments. We have lots of arrows in our quiver, whatever the type or diagnosis for cancer or heart disease. We are extending lifetimes and expectations greatly, and continuously. Increasingly persons are living to be a hundred.

Friends, you and I are standing at a crossroad that is requiring us to make some awesome life or death choices about the future of medical care. The splendid work at Texas Medical Center, as well as the sacrifices of countless volunteers, gifts of buildings, endowed chairs that cost fortunes, and heroism of healthcare volunteer armies <u>are in danger of being trashed by the pettifogging politicians and predator lawyers</u> in Washington, DC and Austin playpens fantasizing that they are benefactors choosing life for us, when in fact they are worse than hired thieves having a grand time choosing matters of life and death for working citizens.

Before we allow the government to choose death by default for *"we the people,"* let's remember how the history of our healthcare evolved, not only at the Texas Medical Center in Houston but also throughout our nation. We want to choose life and hope, especially the Christian hope that does not disappoint us!

Bless you and thank you, doctors, medical personnel, and volunteers by the thousands!

<u>Work</u> and <u>fight on</u>, Texas Medical Center patients, physicians, and your marvelous associated institutions!

Don't give up to the pettifogging politicians and predator lawyers, especially those in Washington, DC. Here in Texas let us work and pray for a future of Heath Care that repudiates Socialized Medicine. Focus your giving and your work relative to medical progress. Keep the Faith.

7. Texas Weather with or without Water

"If you don't like Texas' weather, wait twenty minutes" is a tired aphorism we've all heard many times. With a corollary I'll add, "If you don't like Texas climate, drive a couple hundred miles, but be sure to stay in Texas." Our state has awesome variety of weather, starting in the distant South where the Rio Grande oozes into the Gulf of Mexico, with its near tropical heat most years. In the Panhandle you have the usual four seasons, compounded by so-called blue northers, known in other areas as cold fronts, that slam down from the North Pole when they want to.

A friend once said of his little boys, "They have two speeds; slow and stop." Let me adapt that thought and say that Houston has two temperatures: hot and steamy hot. That may not be quite fair, but it's not far off either. In past years I referred to Houston's "annual week of winter" when temperatures hung out in the 50s or 40s, perhaps even freezing a night or two, but last year we didn't have any winter, not even one night cold enough to build a fire in our fireplace. The AC was on for ten months. About every five years or so, it might snow enough for kids to scrape together a snowball, and schools will let out for an unplanned holiday. Growing numbers of Texans have found their way to ski lifts in Colorado and New Mexico, much of which was formerly parts of Texas.

The real extremes of Texas weather tend to center around rainfall or lack of it from West to East. Extremes range from single-digit average annual moisture in El Paso to over 60 inches average at Orange and the lower Sabine River area. Ranchers in West Texas are always anxious to get as much moisture as they possibly can in any form. Almost no one in far West Texas can imagine the concept of too much rain, such as a flood, until they have one. Ranchers who made it through the drought of the 1950s in banker's parlance describe annual rainfall as dropping "to the low single digits." At the annual Bloys Camp Meeting, where our family went some summers as guests of Mr. J.W. Espy, the ranchers' prayers for rain compared in earnestness with those of the prophet Elijah.

It happens my mother was born in Tucson, Arizona, a place even hotter and drier than El Paso. When our family moved from El Paso to San Antonio, we had three times as much "rain", and Mother considered it an event when she could drive her old Chrysler with all windows open. Her neighbors must have thought she was plumb crazy. That was before the days of automotive air conditioning.

Though the rest of our nuclear family continue to live happily in San Antonio, with Dad's move in 1952 to head up National Bank of Commerce there, I had no idea what a paradigm shift I was in for in 1958 when this "prodigal son" chose to "go East young man." Sometimes Houston gets three times as much rain during a hurricane as El Paso will get in two years. In my collection of Texas books I have one entitled *The Time It Never Rained*.

Every self-respecting Texas town has a "war story" to tell that's a one-hundred-year flood plain event. There was a restaurant in Lampasas that I suppose still has the floodline painted high on their plate glass front window with the note, "It came to here."

Sanderson, Texas surely has its "war story." Dad's friend, Johnny Williams, owned a wool warehouse next to Highway 90. By a freak of nature the summer of 1964, a super heavy rain dumped on the rocky hills above town, and the water cascaded down through Mr. Williams' warehouse like a dose of salts through an old widow.

Sacked wool and mohair rode the crest of the tidal wave through downtown Sanderson, on to the Rio Grande and beyond, most all of it irrecoverable. This was in the days when almost no one thought of flood insurance. Lost in the flood were Mr. William's records, who owned how much wool, or was it mohair?

No one knew what page of the book they were on, so what next?

Anyone for Kings ex? Force majeure? Bankruptcy?

Not on your life.

Mr. Williams promptly set up office in the cab of his pickup, and met with each of his customers to try to figure out the amount of wool or mohair each had prior to the flood; parties hoping for a satisfactory compromise.

Essentially it came down to Mr. Williams accepting the figures of most customers on his bailment, even without the formality of warehouse receipts. In the Texas tradition of a "man's word is his bond," Johnny Williams fully repaid every man without lawsuits and without "government aid."

In the late '50s when I moved to Houston, I didn't have

to wait long to learn about hurricanes. I got to encounter a really big one in 1959, Hurricane Audrey.

That was at a time when I was still wandering in the petrochemical wilderness trying to sell dry ice and chlorine gas to small towns' water works, even some east of the Sabine River. One morning as I was driving to Lake Charles in my rattle-trap 1946 Ford, the radio program was interrupted to give warning of a hurricane expected to make landfall in a couple of hours near Cameron, La.

"That's due south of where I am!," I said to myself. Though it was mid-morning, I decided it would be best to get indoors, so I pulled into the next "tourist court" as we used to call them. What I witnessed that morning from inside the tourist court was the ferocity of Mother Nature, such as I had neither seen before nor since. I experienced Hurricane Audrey in the midst of torrential rain and semi-darkness, coupled with winds clocked at over 100 miles per hour that whipsawed the large steel sign on the tourist court. But it never came off its mooring. Extremely high winds picked up again following the period of near quiet when the eye of the storm passed over us, but what I witnessed from my motel window was child's play compared with the damage Audrey heaped on Cameron, Louisiana, 20 miles to my south.

After a time, the wind and rain decreased as Audrey made its way straight at us in Westlake, Louisiana! People began to venture outside. Gradually the locals realized communication had been lost with the town of Cameron. Phones were out. There were no cell phones then. There was no power. Why was there no word from Cameron, Louisiana?

It would be another day before the picture began to emerge of Audrey's damage, surely not a pretty one. Most folks got word of the storm, <u>except that 10 percent</u> who never do. Weather forecasting then was less than a science, so neither the direction nor force of the hurricane could be determined until it was too late.

Hour by hour as day two emerged, news of the death toll climbed steadily, together with horror stories of drownings and encounters face to face with water moccasins. Soon the death toll passed 100. By the third day it passed 200, then 300 and ultimately over 400 confirmed deaths resulted from Hurricane Audrey.

While not in league with the estimated 6,000 – 12,000 deaths that resulted from the Galveston Hurricane of 1900, the deadliest hurricane in US history, Hurricane Audrey of 1960 was big and she was bad. The most terrible aspect of it was that nearly all loss of life might have been prevented <u>*had those persons taken weather reports seriously and evacuated early*</u>.

Though I failed to be thankful at the time, I was fortunate to have survived Audrey. With named hurricanes, a good rule to remember and implement is this: *overreact early*.

More important, far more important concerning hurricanes, wherever you are in Texas, forget that you ever heard the tired saying about waiting twenty minutes for a weather change. That's not the way it works.

Overreact *immediately*!

Move out, if you can; otherwise, *take the highest cover* nearby.

8. Cowboys Now and Then

The cowboy mystique fascinates us as much today as it did people in the 20th century, long after the frontier closed in 1890, though distribution and concentration of cowboys has changed considerably.

Now well into the 21st century, the romance of the cowboy still rides high. How does this happen?

The Fat Stock Show and Rodeo in Houston is a bigger attraction than ever, held now in Reliant Stadium where over 2 million folks (specifically 2,262,834) came in 2011, exceeding the records set during Astrodome years. Night after night for three weeks, people will pull on their boots and Levis, put on their hats and pull out their wallets to go see the animals and celebrities. But most go to watch today's cowboys perform both in and outside the rodeo arena.

What's your opinion of rodeos? Which events do you enjoy most of all: calf roping? bull riding? steer wrestling? calf scramble? All require both strength and skill   calf roping requires the most skill, bull riding and steer wrestling take the most strength, as in brute strength, even gladiatorial strength.

In my El Paso days, I saw enough rodeos to last a lifetime, but I never participated, only watched. I value my health and respect my body. I'm neither a wimp nor a sissy. In candor I think most rodeo events tend more toward self-abuse than male chauvinism. Some of the boys that I grew up with were into rodeo'n (translation: trying to make a living from winnings generated on the rodeo circuit). The guys I remember are dead now, prematurely.

One neat event that includes skill, beauty, and precision is the women's barrel races, though it probably started as a sop to women from that consummate expression of "male chauvinism" and/or "macho syndrome," the rodeo. An event open to pre-teens only but providing the audience with lots of laughs is the calf scramble. Once at an amateur rodeo in the Hill Country, we let our boys enter the contest when they were kids. Fortunately they didn't bring home a calf, because it would have been a problem to take care of, even with Live Oak Ranch.

For years Dad Smith was an active member of the venerable Texas and Southwestern Cattle Raisers Association, which has a strong working relationship with the Texas Rangers. Once when no one was at Live Oak Ranch, a thief broke into our saddle barn and stole six saddles, together with bridles, blankets and halters. When Dad discovered the break-in, he was heartsick, especially since a couple of the saddles had been given him by his two greatest mentors, Mr. Flory and Mr. J. W. Espy.

Well, Dad called the sheriff of Comal County, who leisurely drove out to the ranch, offered sympathy and a few laconic comments. Since one tip of Live Oak Ranch juts into Kendall County, Dad decided to call the sheriff in Boerne, too. Results were about the same, nothing but sympathy.

Next morning Dad had a great idea. Remembering the Texas Cattlemen's special relationship with the Texas Rangers, he called Austin and reported the theft, neither of cattle nor horses, but the next closest thing to them, *saddles*. In less than two hours a Ranger was at Live Oak Ranch, notebook in hand, as wide awake as a third baseman and full of questions.

Back in San Antonio the following week, Dad got a call from a Ranger. "Mr. Smith, this is Ranger (such-and-such), and I'm calling from a pawn shop here on South Zarzamora Street. Could you please come down here to confirm that these are your saddles and bridles?"

Eureka!
Justice had prevailed!
Texas Rangers to the rescue!

The thief was apprehended, tried, convicted, and sentenced to a few months in Huntsville. It turned out he was a neighbor turned thief, which was perverse, disgusting, and disappointing.

This rodeo season I've worn my cowboy boots three days and my top-of-the-line Stetson hat once. My boots are custom made and well shined, a gift from years ago from nephews expressing thanks for Espy Deer Hunts through the years. My Stetson dates from our days in chemical trucking when we gave the hats as a premium for driving carefully with no tickets, accidents, and/or no driving on flat tires.

Back to the subject of cowboy mystique, "Where," you might ask, "are the authentic cowboys in this 21st century, the ones making their living punching cattle?" Good question!

Are they an endangered species? Should we be organizing a group to preserve authentic cowboys the way Greenies organize in order to preserve snail darters or endangered species of horned toads?

Search me!

There are surely some authentic cowboys out there, but they grow fewer each year.

In my days in El Paso there was a clear distinction between "drugstore cowboys" and the real thing, that is, those making their living in the cattle business usually with working ranches. In the 20th century, if you or I wore boots, hats, and Levis, we'd have been referred to with the pejorative "drugstore cowboy" translation: "pretend cowboy." "Cowpuncher" was the authentic term of fraternity membership among authentic cowboys.

Back then there was a character from an authentic ranching family near El Paso who was considered by many folks to be a lazy cowboy. It was said that he punched more cattle in the lobby of the Paso del Norte Hotel, talking incessantly mostly to tourists, than he ever had on his family ranch.

Most county seat towns in Texas used to have cattle auction barns that were a center of action weekdays. As time went by the cattle barns dropped down to opening only a couple of days a week, then finally in most towns they closed permanently. Last count of 254 Texas' counties, only 24 had viable cattle auction barns.

On sale days city slickers and owners of small ranches would gather to buy or sell a few head at the auction barn, each considering himself a superior judge of cattle when he would raise his hand to the auctioneer and shout his higher bid, "twenty-seven" to which the auctioneer might shout back "twenty-seven, twenty-seven, gobba, gobba, getta, gobba, who'll give me twenty-eight? Twenty-eight, who'll give twenty-eight?" "Twenty-nine?"

And so this jibber jabber would persist until "Sold!" was shouted with the fall of a wooden mallet. The buyer was usually a man in Levis, boots, and a Stetson, but more recently that "cowboy" just might have been a dentist from Houston. Whoever he was, he probably had a lot of tall explaining to do to his wife at dinner if he didn't have a place to run his cattle, now that he had "started his own herd."

When I was a boy growing up in West Texas, the farm-ranch component of our GNP was probably 30 percent; today it's scarcely one percent and dropping.

In the '50s, Texas suffered a drought on par with the disaster of the Great Flood of 1927 nationally. But an important difference between the flood of '27 and our Texas drought of the '50s is that the drought lasted a long time, like five years! The effect on ranchers was tragic: having to buy feed at inflated prices or, as an alternate, selling your cattle at the auction barn at prices depressed by so many other authentic ranchers who were experiencing the same problems. For many ranchers it was heroic if they could just pay their taxes in order to hold onto their ranches a little longer. Many couldn't, and lost their places kept for generations in one family that went to the tax collector or the highest bidder. Sad.

To this day I remember the ranchers' prayers for rain during the Bloys Camp Meeting held near Fort Davis. Their fervor would have rivaled that of the prophet Elijah praying for rain. Mr. J. W. Espy, Dad's mentor and best customer at State National Bank, used to encourage fellow ranchers by saying, "The cattle business is gonna' come back. It'll come back. But we have to help make it come back!" Mr. Espy believed in both adrenalin and prayer, an excellent paradox to embrace, ranchers and theologians as well.

Let me amplify on him, for his was a lifestyle worth emulating, especially these days when even our year-to-date rain total in Houston (as of September 2011) is still a single digit. Mr. Espy was the epitome of a West Texas rancher type: winsome, honest to the core, hard-working and possessing a good sense of humor. He moved to Fort Davis at the turn of the 20th century, with small capital and less than a high school education, and spent his life building up seven ranches with herds of cattle to match. More than just a cowboy, he was an authentic cowpuncher, and even more, a full-time, bona-fide cattleman. He was one of the founding members of the Bloys Camp Meeting Association and a staunch supporter of the Southwestern Children's Home. He was also like a daddy to my daddy, Dad Smith.

Looking back at Dad buying Live Oak Ranch and my own three misadventures in ranching, I've decided that the cowboy mystique must be inherited through the male genes of our species. Do you suppose?

Let me tell you about cattle economics.

- It was basically uneconomical when Dad ran Herefords and played at ranching the last third of his life. But more important, what a great place Live Oak Ranch is for his extended family, except those believing in non-verbal communications that boycott it.

- During the years that I leased Powell Ranch near Fort Davis, I lost money on the ranching side of the operation but it was more than worth it for the extraordinary fun we had sponsoring the traditional annual Espy Deer Hunts (mule deer, not white tails) the week after Thanksgiving each year.

- Let me mention another episode about losing money ranching. Though the CXI Ranch's coal investment near Longview proved uneconomical in the 1970s, I somehow thought we could make incremental revenue raising cattle. WRONG! I should say wrong again, even a third time! (Things like this convince me I'm a slow learner.)

It took a Dutch Uncle approach by Bob Kautzman, Les Moor, and my financial officer Les Jeko to convince me that you must have several factors in place to make even a modest living ranching. I list them for the benefit of others who might be infatuated with the cowboy mystique and who fantasize that because it's so wonderful they might be able to make two and two equal seven or more.

Well, here's to trying. To make even a marginal living ranching <u>or otherwise putting feed through bovines to make beef</u> (except feedlots), you must do <u>all</u> these things:

1. Own your ranch and operate it free of any debt.
2. Run at least 400 units (cows only, not counting the cows with calves).
3. Work at least 55 hours a week, <u>yourself</u>.
4. Be able personally to make all mechanical repairs; i.e., vehicles, motors, wells, cutters, et al. (Apologies: I'm a mechanical moron. Deal me out.)

5. Limit veterinary bills to say $2000 a year.

6. Don't have more than one ranchhand / swamper / roustabout / migrant worker / wetback, who must also be infatuated with the cowboy mystique lifestyle and will work hard (grunt work) for a bunk, meals of mostly beans, bread and coffee, plus a salary of maybe $225 per week.

If you can get all six of these squirrels up one tree at one time consistently for five years, one of which will be negative cash flow, you might, emphasis _might_, average $25,000/year net to the bottom line. Please understand that this is your bottom, bottom line   that is, there is no "salary" on top of it, no "bonus," and no dollops.

Now.

A far better alternate is to first save $250 cash for annual "rodeo'n."   Then go down to one of the western wear stores around Houston, Galena Park, or any other of the five major cities in Texas, and let them "do you" or even "do you in." Then head to the Fat Stock Show and Rodeo in your outfitted hat, boots, bright shirt, Levis, with a package of Bull Durham hanging out of your shirt pocket (display purposes only).

It's okay to go to a rodeo once at least once a year, whether you're feeling well or not.

Footnote: It happens that I have a lifetime friend with the unique name of Weston Ware who I hope will join me in setting up a partnership business at Galena Park named "Weston Ware Western Wear."

See us in Galena Park for all your Cowboy Western Wear needs.

ADVENTURES OF THE EARLY YEARS

9. Espy Deer Hunt

Some things among life's adventures are so fine that we want to share them with our friends. Such for me was mule deer hunting in the Davis Mountains of far West Texas where for some fifty years we aggressively hunted those craggy mountains and awesome canyons on horseback. Let me tell you about it.

When I was a little boy growing up in El Paso, the finest thing I could conceive of was to be invited mule deer hunting on Mr. J. W. Espy's huge ranch north of Fort Davis, Texas. Dad was cashier at State National Bank in El Paso, and among his loan customers the finest was Mr. J.W. Espy. He was the epitome of a West Texas rancher, always as good as his word, winsome, hardworking, and in those years, prosperous. Mr. Espy and Dad did many good cattle loans together since Dad was de facto the Ranch Loan Department at State National Bank.

The Epsy Deer Hunt was held during the 10-day mule deer season after Thanksgiving for family and friends of Mr. Espy, which included my Dad. The year I turned 12, I got invited, too.

Wow!

Talk about an impressive rite of passage! I could hardly wait for the Friday after Thanksgiving and the four hour drive to Espy Ranch, where by nightfall some dozen hunters assembled.

For a week we would get up at 5 a.m. to the ranch cook's clanger gong, eat a hearty breakfast cooked over open coals, mount our horses, and move out before daylight. Days would be action packed as we worked the high ridges where bucks might hide.

That first year as a 12-year old I took a lot of kidding from Mr. Espy's two sons Jim and Clay, who teased one another and their guests as well, and certainly me as the new kid on the hunt. One joke was for Mr. Frank Jones to pretend to be the game warden, find a serious problem with my hunting license and then arrest me.

The hunting was both intense and strenuous, dismounting to look for deer, and then usually remounting unless we got a shot. I remember one late afternoon getting off my horse at Auja Springs for a drink doubting that I could get back on. I was exhausted and painfully sore, but I did get back on my also tired horse.

And I'll always remember shooting my first buck late one morning off Short Canyon amidst hoot-haws and shouts from the Espy boys, who then treated me like I was a hero when I got a three point spike buck my third shot, using old Mr. Flory's Winchester 30-30. Today we still have that 1894 lever action repeating rifle which is a collector's item, at least for me.

Mr. Flory, Dad's boss, had gone on the very first Espy Deer Hunt in 1929. He gave Dad that 30-30, which Dad ultimately passed on to me. One day I'll pass it on to Davo Jr., or more correctly, David M. Smith IV.

After supper with tables cleared, out would come the

poker chips for three tables of poker. Inside was the game for grown men only, casually but firmly governed by Mr. Espy. You played only if you chose to and knew the ranch rules on poker. You were limited to three raises. Anyone losing $100 had to drop out lest "family relations" jeopardize your coming back in future years. At the ranch house in the side bedroom there was a table with much lower stakes, "penny ante poker" as it's called, though the ante was a nickel (inflation you know). Outside in the cook shed was the third game where novices, especially first timers, and the cooks plus ranch hands played with matchsticks for stakes.

Since my first hunt in 1944, I have been out to Espy Ranch the day after Thanksgiving almost every year except my two years in the United States Army. During those two years my commanding officer, a snotty captain, informed me that I could go on my all-important mule deer hunt if I insisted, but that on return I would face court-martial charges of AWOL (absence without leave.)

In the years since about 1903 old Mr. Espy had assembled several ranches totaling over 100,000 acres, and each of his daughters got a ranch when he died. The former Powell Ranch, where our hunts started, became the Williams Ranch, which I later leased until 1990. It was my good fortune to share the great fun and exhausting pleasure of each season's Espy Deer Hunt with about a dozen people for many years, giving a horseback mule deer hunt to over 200 friends and many of their sons, most of whom got their first mule deer buck on my Espy Deer Hunt.

The late Texas artist Mark Storm was one special guest that I had out several times to Espy Ranch. Three of

Mark's original paintings that I own are scenes on the Powell. "In Sight of the House" pictures me and Dad Smith returning to the ranch headquarters late one fall afternoon. Dad loved to use the expression, "We're in sight of the house, Davo", which I heard numerous times when we could in fact see the ranch (yellow speck) with my buck's carcass over a saddle horn. My second Mark Storm painting, "Buying the Ranch," encompasses the occasion when Mr. Espy and Mr. Powell made their deal from some high point near the start of Short Canyon. They had arrived at a tentative agreement on terms of purchase, and because of the size and formality of the transaction they had stopped so that Mr. Espy could write up the terms and details on a wrapper that accompanied each package of Bugler Pipe Tobacco.

"Losing the Way" depicts a memorable event when one of my guests shot a buck off Viejo Canyon as it was getting dark. I had dismounted to try finding that buck in that longest defile of Short Canyon. Daylight got away from me as I proceeded slowly down the defile.

Knowing that my own horse would wander back home the next day, I went in the canyon, which I knew joined the main road to ranch headquarters two or three miles further. Cat claw and Spanish Dagger were all around me with no room but to squat. Without moonlight it was pitch dark.

By throwing a rock I could tell I was on a steep incline.

I was alone. I was the next thing to being lost. . . .

Uncomfortable and cold, I got to spend most of that night on one spot in that defile until after midnight.

Ultimately I heard a faint call from someone far down Short Canyon. . . .

It was James Green. . . . "Dave...oh. . . . !"

There was hope! Then there was a vehicle horn from way down Short Canyon, and soon a tiny light appeared!

I shouted, **"I'M... UP... HERE!"**

I was still in the land of the living. Better still, sooner rather than later I was back at the ranch house sitting in front of a warm fire sipping coffee and telling Mike's and my story, since it was Mike's buck that I had tried to locate for over two hours, unsuccessfully prowling through the dense brush.

Mark Storm's grandson and family are still active members of Houston's South Main Baptist Church. Together we continue our search for any or all of Mark Storm's original paintings that we might find in order to reproduce, as well as one day assemble in a book to be titled, "Works of Mark Storm." So far we have made little progress toward this goal.

In any case I have enough good memories of the Espy Deer Hunt to last a lifetime. Many old hunting friends also have great memories to recall as well, though a growing number of those friends have died.

In my advanced middle age, I sometimes fantasize about trying to buy a small West Texas ranch in the Davis Mountains like Espy Ranch, especially to share the breathtaking views from Texas' rooftop. On clear days our vistas from peaks on the Davis Mountains, especially Star Mountain, allow us views to see 50 miles and more... Pecos... Balmorhea... Black Mountain... Mitre Peak... Wild Rose Pass... Star Mountain... Swayback...

All of it is Glorious!

10. Avalanche!

During my pre-teen years, my parents decided that I too should take piano lessons like my brothers had before me. Forrest Jr. or "Buddy," the oldest of us three Smith boys and musically the smartest, had made rapid progress in his years with Mrs. Ponsford of Morgan Studios. He showed ability early to play by ear, sailing through the pieces such as Falling Waters, Indian Song, and The Happy Farmer. Paul or "Bim," next older, also did reasonably well with Mrs. Ponsford's piano lessons.

Then my mother faced a problem. She found it hard to accept the fact that the musical genes that kicked out liberally in Buddy, and moderately in Bim, came out negligibly in Davo.

At the end of my first year with Mrs. Ponsford, I had barely made it through "Falling Waters" or whatever it was that I played at the Spring Recital. I wasn't tone deaf like a couple of my buddies but then neither did I have perfect pitch. Mother just would not accept the fact that I was doing poorly. Apparently a heavy decision was made behind closed doors at Morgan Studios, though not in a smoke-filled room. Davo Smith, for reasons expedient, would have a different music teacher after summer vacation.

It occurred to me that what was going on was comparable to punting at football. When the prospect of losing the whole game is imminent, you punt! This makes for big changes, and though you likely lose control of the ball, you still might catch up and win. Another executive decision made for me was that instead of Mrs. Ponsford, I would have Mrs. Learmonth, a teacher who made "house calls", as they used to say of doctors. (I got the message that my case must have been serious.)

It happens that Mrs. Learmonth was also paid organist for Peak Hagadon Funeral Home, which compounded the problems whenever she taught this dullard following a funeral. Mrs. Learmonth definitely lacked professional detachment. I can hear her now trying to teach me between sobs: "Boo-hoo-hoo. Now, Davo, curve those fingers, boo-hoo-hoo-hoo-hoo." It even crossed my mind that my performance or lack thereof just might have been the proximate cause of Mrs. Learmonth's profuse crying, compounded by funerals.

Whether there was learning progress or not that year is doubtful. But as winter receded, plans were made for the Spring Recital by students of Morgan Studios, to be held at the Women's Club of El Paso, high on Mesa Hill.

Another Executive Session was likely held at Morgan Studios to which I was not privy, that must have gone something like this:

"Davo Smith has not progressed past "Falling Waters.""

"Not only does he not learn; he doesn't even practice."

"Perhaps if we were to put Davo Smith with Mrs. Learmonth's super star student Don Henry, we might, by means of a two piano piece *average up* for Davo but also cover his ineptness," (Mrs. Morgan, ostensibly the speaker).

There was another unspoken consideration that

hopefully this youngest Smith boy would move on to other things not musical and all would be well.

The two piano piece chosen for me to play at the Spring Recital had an ominous even prophetic title:

AVALANCHE!

But the biggest problem for me was that the kid at the other piano for the pending *AVALANCHE* was to be Don Henry, my buddy Charles Henry's *little* brother.

"So what?" you ask.

So plenty!

Though he may have been a musical genius, that twerp was Charles Henry's *little* brother.

(You always translated the word "little" as in "little brother" as "inferior".)

I wasn't about to waste time helping Charles Henry's *little* brother show off his musical smarts.

Weeks passed and we were making no progress. More correctly, *I* was making no progress. Don Henry didn't have to make any progress since he was so far out in front of me in that he could "sight read." Whether or not I curved my fingers, I doubt that Mrs. Learmonth could find many teachable moments in our humorless, dreadful, weekly hour together.

I liked doing more important things with Don's big brother Charles, like using parents' flashlights to explore the experimental caves in Mount Franklin dug by students from the College of Mines and Metallurgy nearby, or hiking over to the AS&R plant at Smelter Lake. Timing for such important events conflicted with music lessons, occasionally causing what our YMCA club, the Pioneers, used to call a calculated fumble.

March and half of April got away from us with no progress on my part of the impending *AVALANCHE* duo. Don Henry had aced his part of the duo, the hard part.

Mrs. Learmonth implored my mom to urge her darling Davo (she really didn't call me that) to practice, so that the cleverly conceived *AVALANCHE* in two parts would come off or come down as planned.

I'm sure a fitting word of warning, translate threat, from Dad Smith would have had a tonic effect on my attitude but curiously it was not forthcoming until it was too late.

Mother implored me to practice, and I got down to business seriously the last week before the recital. Using what I call the hammer/anvil/ramrod method of education, (i.e. sheer repetition), I fragilely learned my part of *AVALANCHE*," or so I thought.

Two days before recital, Don Henry and I managed to play through the complete *AVALANCHE* once, only once, without having it come down on *us*.

D DAY for the recital was a Saturday afternoon late in May. We performers peeking from behind the curtains could see mothers, brothers, and grandparents assembling in the auditorium. I clearly remember that we were third on the program. An announcement was made over the sound system. "Next on the program we have Don Henry and Davo Smith, playing a two piano number . . . . *AVALANCHE*."

Looking back from today's vantage point, I recall Custer's words prior to the fateful battle of Little Big Horn: "Up men and to your posts!" The two of us walked onstage to polite applause, faced a sea of happy faces, bowed seriously and took our posts, each seated at a piano.

I led off hesitantly,

    ta-ta-ta, ta-ta-ta, taaaaaa....

Don answered confidently,

    ta-ta-ta, ta-ta-ta, ta-ta-ta, ta,ta-ta,

    ta-ta-ta, ta-ta-ta, room ta-ta-ta, taaaaa.

(So far so good; my second part repeated the first)

    ta-ta-ta, ta-ta-ta, taaaaaa....

Don responded elegantly,

    room ta-ta-ta-ta- room ta-ta-ta-ta,

    room ta-ta-ta-ta, taaaaaa...

Tenuously we completed the first half of *AVALANCHE* and then moved into the second half, where we were supposed to play both jointly... and harmoniously.

Instead, Divergence and Discord crept in. . . . !

Pretending confidence I grabbed an idea, a bad one, and kept right on playing, though noticeably off track. The *AVALANCHE* was beginning to come down on us!!

Accusingly, I glared at Don Henry, Charles Henry's *little* brother, with a feigned arrogance that as much as said, "That little twerp caused all of this trouble!" I plowed on, but headlong as if it were very heavy snow of avalanche proportions.

Then Mrs. Morgan had to come on stage, gesturing *"STOP!... STOP!"*

Too bad she didn't have an umpire's whistle to blow, calling off the game. I must have just shrugged my shoulders, supposing by nonverbal communication to ask, "Is something wrong here?"

If there was any doubt as to my musical inability following my first year recital of "Falling Waters," there surely was none following my disastrous performance of

AVALANCHE.

Perhaps if they'd given grades on *interpretation*, the **non-musical aspects** of my unique rendition of *AVALANCHE* might have earned me an "A." I may not have brought down the house with applause or laughs, but I did give the folks at Morgan Studio something more of an "avalanche" than anyone ever expected, or has likely brought on before or since.

In my head and in my heart I knew neither my older brothers nor my Mother had been fooled that May afternoon.

I hadn't fooled Mrs. Learmonth, Mrs. Morgan, nor Mrs. Ponsford either.

Only one person was fooled that day, and it wasn't Don Henry, Charles Henry's *little* brother.

You guessed it.

It was Davo Smith.

Though I was too old to be tucked in by Mother, she came in that night to do prayers, and we had a little talk.

I asked, "Mom, do I *really* have to take piano lessons again next year?"

"No," she answered kindly, "you really don't have to."

That I *really* appreciated my mother's response is an understatement.

Had the case been turned over to a "higher court", shall we say, the outcome would certainly have been far more like an actual...

AVALANCHE.

11. The Undertaker Comes for David Smith

When I was a freshman at The University of Texas, my big brother Bim's good friend Dave Gardner invited me squirrel hunting west of Austin at the fraternity lake club. Having been mule deer hunting every year since I was twelve, I figured squirrel hunting might be some fun and an adventure, albeit with smaller game, squirrels instead of mule deer, Fiji woods instead of the awesome Espy Ranch, and .22s instead of 30-30s.

I was right, but for the wrong reasons. It was surely an adventure but ended up being a brush with death, not for the squirrel, _but for me_. Here's the story.

At the Fiji Lake Club, Dave Gardner and I loaded our .22s and went into the woods, slowly walking in tandem, well apart, looking up in the trees for squirrels. We had not gone far when I felt something hit me above my left ankle, surely more than an insect bite.

I had stepped on a snake!

There he was, red and slithering, definitely a poisonous treacherous copperhead that unlike the rattlesnake, gives no warning before it strikes.

I shouted to Dave to come quickly, and then put a shell in the chamber and killed the snake.

Dave Gardner was probably more scared than I was. I had never been even a tenderfoot in Boy Scouts, but I knew how to make a tourniquet, which we did with a long sleeve and a stout stick. Then Dave took out his pocket knife, fortunately sharp, and with trembling hand cut an X where the copperhead had struck me, just above my right ankle bone. After that he sucked a lot of blood and spit it out, which was the accepted treatment for poisonous snake bites at the time.

I had no feeling in my lower right leg because of the tourniquet. Dave helped me hobble back to the car and we headed for Seton Hospital, Dave speeding while I held the stick to keep the tourniquet tight.

The doctor on duty at Seton Hospital was manifestly untrained. He wanted to be helpful, yet he came across not at all sure of himself, like trying to throw darts at a target in a dark room. He sent for a large dose of antivenin and mentioned after reading the directions that it might, just might cause an allergic reaction in some people, perhaps one in a hundred, if that person was allergic to horse serum. He gave me a shot of whatever the serum and kept me overnight, intending to send me "home" to Brackenridge Dormitory at the University. I was feeling fair.

But three nights later the horse serum that was the carrier for the antivenin hit me like a ton of bricks. I had drawn the black bean. I was that "one in a hundred" allergic to horse serum!

My lips, my eyelids, ear lobes, and other soft body parts were swollen. My back was covered with welts   hives, as some people call them. Joe ran downstairs to the pay phone to contact the doctor who told him to call an ambulance and get me to Seton Hospital.

What happened next one might call "gallows humor." At the time it sure wasn't funny to me. I felt as though I was about to die; and, I was.

In the late 1950s it was permissible for undertakers to operate both an ambulance business and a funeral parlor together, which today would be too big a conflict of interest. When Joe called Cook Funeral Home, he learned its ambulance was out on another call. The only person on duty at that hour was an embalmer with but one vehicle available, a long black funeral hearse used to transport corpses. Apparently the embalmer (we'll call him Malcolm) decided it was expedient to come after me in the hearse, so as not to miss any business.

I responded to the rap on the door, "Who is it?"

"I'm Malcolm Passmore with the Cook Funeral Home, and I've come for David Smith," he said in cascading funereal tones.

Adrenalin kicked in. I raised myself and said, "Look, mister, I'm pretty sick, but don't you touch me. And if you think I'm gonna be one of your customers, you're plumb crazy."

Joe returned to our dorm room in time to help me down to the hearse. I insisted on sitting upright in the front seat and off we went to Seton Hospital, me angry, sullen and feeling horrible but intently watching the undertaker drive the hearse. We checked in at the hospital and were directed to an elevator, since it seemed that I could walk, but weakness overtook me and I ended up sitting on the floor. That's when I asked myself and, most importantly, God, "Has my time come?"

By the grace of God, I gradually got better, and in two

or three more days felt nearly well, for which I was profoundly grateful.

Around the Phi Gam house I got a new nickname, "Snake." Fortunately it didn't stick for long.

Then a few weeks later, during a fraternity retreat at Mo Ranch, some of the boys played a trick on me relative to my snakebite experience. They found a small harmless garter snake and put it on my chest one afternoon while I was napping. (I'm good at naps, a skill inherited from my grandfather, David Smith.)

The boys' laughter woke me up. Startled, indeed terrified by the garter snake, I jumped up and drop kicked the steel cot next to mine, bruising my shin while the other boys roared with laughter. They sure got more than just a rise out of me. I had had one encounter with a snake and I didn't want another one. As the old saying goes, "Bit once, cautious twice." Who was it that said, "All's well that ends well?" I guess it was Shakespeare, wasn't it? Well, maybe a good joke once in a while, even at your own expense is okay.

But I'm sure glad that when I stepped on the copperhead that bit me, it was not the end that might have ended my earthly life those many years ago at The University of Texas, at Austin.

12. Bless our Fraternity

When I went off to The University in the fall of 1949 (today UT-Austin), I was pretty well pumped up by family, my brothers especially, to expect something great, even *awesome*. Just what that was to be, was unclear, though more than once my dad had expressed regret that he did not accept an offer from our Great Aunt Lizzie in Jefferson to lend him money to go to The University of Texas. At that time there was one and only one University of Texas, or if you prefer, The University of Texas, although soon about every town with a population of 50,000 or large enough to have a Burger King has a branch of The University and/or now the parallel system out of Texas A&M.

Once or twice I had ridden with my folks the long six hundred miles by car from El Paso to Austin to check on my older brothers, Forrest Jr. (Buddy) and Paul (aka Bim). We would eat Sunday dinner at their fraternity house. The boys wore ties. I called them "sir." Two or three times they'd sing fraternity songs in three-part harmony that sounded hymn-like during the lunch hour. I was properly impressed.

My blood brother Buddy, who was five years older than me, joined Phi Gamma Delta on his return from the Navy, a fraternity of one of Dad's golfing buddies. Buddy was drawn to the ritual, the Greek letters, the secrets, and the special symbols, passwords, handshakes, all laced with

Greek words and other inane nonsense. He was so into fraternity that the Army expression "Gung Ho" comes to mind from Infantry days. Buddy was a UT pre-med senior when he pioneered the new Phi Gamma Delta chapter at LSU in Baton Rouge. Forrest Jr. (Buddy) at that time was referred to by a Greek word, which I've forgotten, for "missionary" from Texas, I suppose, to the less civilized brethren at LSU across the Neches River in Louisiana.

The fall of 1949 when I entered UT, my older brother Paul (Bim) was president of the UT chapter. I was to enter "rush," a curious process by which fraternities add members, which was then in full swing. It seemed to me as phony as a seven dollar bill, but looking back, I guess fraternity members assumed that since I was Frosty and Paul's little brother I would join their fraternity. Without invitation or complaint, and referred to as a "legacy," technically a double legacy. I pretty much went along with the program and soon found myself a "pledge" to an unknown something my brothers somehow thought worthwhile.

Shortly I came to realize that all those fraternity boys were not like my own big brothers. In fact, quite a few of them were closer to the opposite, fine songs and ties at Sunday dinner notwithstanding. One of the members was sadistic to the fraternity dog, throwing him off the second story porch into the bushes to hear him howl. Late one Saturday night a taxi driver pulled up to the fraternity house and essentially dumped a member on the entry floor, dead drunk. One older member who had been in WWII, and who was referred to as our "trainer", had a constant snide outlook. By objective standards he was just plain <u>mean</u>. (I supposed that meant we pledges were to be treated like horses or dogs.)

I began to wonder who these men were that I was associating with. Sure, there were some fine fellows among them, but what was all this secret stuff and jibber-jabber they were making us learn? Some members' relatives were authentic Texas Germans; i.e., pre-World War I and II, had parked their ethnic prejudice/hatred, especially with another war an object to reset their ethnic hatred on.

My roommate Joe Hammond from El Paso and I were at least moderately committed to good school work. Living as we did at Brackenridge Hall near the fraternity house, both of us were pledges and went to the weekly indoctrination sessions. Some of the stuff was fun or funny, like ganging up on a member on his birthday to throw him into Littlefield Fountain or having to stand on your chair and sing your high school "hymn" or fight song. I could handle all that.

Our older ethnic German, quite possible by his constant sneer and hatred vented on us pledges might well have been a U boat commander in another war and time zone.

By snide remarks and other statements we pledges were given to understand that not every pledge would "make it." There were references to previous unknown pledges who *did not make it* for various reasons, such as poor grades (flunking out), but primarily it was for not having the macho stuff to endure "hell week," which was three days of semi-sadistic tests contrived by the less intelligent members for the perverse amusement of certain members. We pledges were made to walk like ducks while the members would pour catsup and drop eggs on us from the fraternity house second story porch at 300 West 27th Street, next door to Austin Presbyterian Theological Seminary.

The climax to "rush" came late one night when some 30 odd members of the "pledge class" were blindfolded, "kidnapped," then dumped at a remote place out in Travis Country. We pledges were left walking around blindfolded in a large circle, singing a ridiculous though not obscene song, while the members sneaked off.

It was at the end of the second day of this asinine nonsense that I decided fraternity was not for me. I hunted up my actual brother Paul and in anger plus disgust expressed my view about as follows; "Bim, I've had enough of this stuff and I'm checking out. I've made a few friends in the pledge class, but if this is brotherhood, then I want none of it." I ranted on even in tears.

Paul (Bim) urged me not to quit, especially since I was only a week from formal initiation and the hazing was nearly over. He reminded me that I would be allowed to enter the third floor chapter hall (translate holy of holies) and would learn the mysteries of full fellowship in my brothers' fraternity. An issue that remained unspoken between us was that both Bim as past president and Buddy, a Gung-Ho "Fiji," would be disappointed and embarrassed were I to quit. With reluctance, I agreed to continue through "hell week."

Did I make a mistake in not carrying out my intended resolve to quit which I expressed to Bim? Possibly so.

(Come to think of it a little more, I'll change my position to "probably so.") As a matter of fact, this may come as something of a surprise, because Bim and I never revisited the issue in the years since I expressed intent *not* to join the Fijis. For all I know, I may be deemed a traitor or at least a heretic by those who may look at me sideways should I attend the annual Fiji reunion at a beer joint in downtown San Antonio. At my advanced middle age I hate to give offense to brothers or shirt tail relatives or my dad's side of the family.

The fact is, or was, I had an identity problem in the fraternity. It was assumed that I, as Frosty Smith's little brother, was likewise enthusiastic about the useless drivel taught to pledges: the mystery, the history, the candles, the Greek names, and the men whose duty it was to ensure that the door to the chapter hall was well guarded. These and other important "secrets" were contained in a book called the *Purple Pilgrim*, which some called the fraternity's "Bible."

Can you imagine yourself in a position of having to teach something you knew to be *false* or even just inane? During my sophomore year at the University of Texas, located in Austin, Texas, I found myself having to teach that perverse stuff of the *Purple Pilgrim* to new pledges, as though it were substantive.

For the record, in Christian candor I'll tell you, actual fathers and brothers in the bond, shirt tail relatives, the whole business of Greek letter college fraternities is flawed.

It just popped into my head that there was one time in my life when something from the *Purple Pilgrim* found its way into a conversation in an interesting way. Years after college and fraternity days, a neat Louisiana school teacher, today my wife, and I were growing interested in one another. Though she was still working on her Masters degree at LSU (where Buddy had gone for a year), she had never heard of the Fijis, but she dazzled me with lots of profoundly useless information such as the latitude and annual rainfall necessary to grow sugar cane on plantations in South Louisiana.

She had invited me to meet her folks in the college town of Hammond, LA. As we were crossing the Mississippi River by ferry into St. Francisville, I took the opportunity to astonish her with some of *my* fraternity knowledge. It went something like this:

"Hmmm, St. Francisville; that's where the immortal Daniel Webster Crofts is buried," I observed casually.

"Who?"

"Daniel Webster Crofts. You know, one of the Immortal Six."

"Immortal Six? Who, might I ask, are the Immortal Six?" she continued.

"Were," I corrected.

"OK, who were they?"

"The founders of the Fijis," I responded as though that were a fact any sixth grade school teacher like Charis Jeanne should know.

She looked at me as if to say, "What have we here?"

We weren't connecting. Charis later told me that she was going down the trail to the Fiji Islands, when what I meant by Fijis were members of the fraternity of Phi Gamma Delta.

I had one more arrow in my quiver to fire and I fired it. But it still wasn't the right one.

"You'll have to read about them in the *Purple Pilgrim*, but much of it is secret," I told her.

Her look of passing curiosity changed to one of anxious concern, especially as we passed by the state mental hospital at Denham Springs, Louisiana. But we still weren't connecting.

What if she had said thank you, but she would go on to Hammond by herself?

Perish the thought!

Fraternity well might be viewed as a stage in life, part of growing up, perhaps like the terrible "twosies" but for nearly grown college boys. There were and are some fine things that came out of the Fijis for me, especially two chemical engineers who joined me in CXI/Texmark several years later as limited partners. But that's a different venue and another story. Unspoken aspects of fraternity life give me a problem. At the risk of being black-balled at the next Fiji Reunion, I'll speak my minority opinion.

To all nephews, great nephews and others interested, for the sake of your own initiative, independence, and freedom of adventure, I would recommend that you *not join a fraternity*; i.e., a Greek letter, college, solely social fraternity.

From possibly so to probably not, let's move this thing still down another notch to probably not. Fraternity was not for me as an average, friendly, West Texas boy, not an offspring from a family of psychological cripples. Who might a single teenage boy from the back of the room at CHAPTER Hall think he is/was when he points his thumb downward and shouts "BALL!"

Friends can be found lots of ways, most of which are far better than rush week, hell week, with or without any of the ritual nonsense that goes with fraternity and/or Purple

Pilgrim equivalent. Consider the unnecessary embarrass-
ment and hurt caused many a young man not accepted in a
fraternity for trifling reasons. Isn't there something
artificial about joining an outfit, paying costly dues,
playing at ritual with attendant jibber-jabber just to have a
few instant "friends?"

When I found myself making a "pledge" to something
supposed to be "my first and all powerful influence and
rule of daily action", it was too much. I was making a
mistake, a commitment to something patently false,
especially in the case of Frosty Smith, my oldest brother
who died a few years ago.

I must tell you with no reservations that my oldest
brother Forrest Moseley Smith, Jr. was a Christian
gentleman, and was well-qualified for a positive hereafter
as any man I know. Risking judgment myself, merely to
say this, but I shall; to voice judgment written with word,
or as a blank marble dropped in a box, borders on, indeed
is, blasphemy.

The *Purple Pilgrim* says that upon death a deceased
member's fraternity pin is supposed to be placed over his
heart, pointing diagonally over his left shoulder.

So far as I know, this detail was overlooked when my
blood brother Buddy was buried in San Antonio.

Do you think we should go over to San Antonio and dig
him up to see if his Fiji pin is pointed diagonally over the
left shoulder of his burial suit of clothes? What if it points
over his right shoulder?

It is here that I must reject fraternity like a foreign body
as it might well be confused with the Christian faith, which
it most emphatically was not and is not, a verse or two of

scripture from Ecclesiastes or other "Old Testament" scripture, notwithstanding to the contrary.

I here and now see need to repudiate my childish pledge to "Fijis" that I _believe_ in <u>Phi Gamma Delta</u>, guide and teacher of my heart.

This is a perversion of the "Apostles Creed" which I can say and here affirm with agape love and candor. To the core of my being I am certain that I would have made other friends during my four years at The University, had I not joined the fraternity; or better yet, with a little more encouragement, gone to A&M! In candor, as expressed elsewhere, I was a closet Aggie. I would have made new friends on my own no matter what school I attended. I am not a wimp, and I am not a psychological cripple.

I have been working on this essay off and on for years now. Brother Bim and I will soon be planning the Men's Luncheon in December for all members and in-laws of Dad Smith. I may share this essay at that time with men 60 years old, plus Smith men or in-laws who will attend, both for their sake as well as others of our extended Smith Family. I'll conclude my with a single word that fraternity men will understand. Regarding membership in any purely social Greek letter fraternity, my vote in Christian candor now or hereafter should be,

BALL!

13. Infantry School as an MBA

Though Dad Smith had but a high school education, he impressed on his three boys the value and importance of all kinds of education and his readiness to pay for graduate school, provided we focused. Buddy (Forrest, Jr.) took Dad's offer, went to medical school at Pennsylvania and became a pediatrician. Paul (Bim) took it as well, went to law school at Texas, passed the bar, and became an attorney;)do not call him a lawyer). Dad suggested that I go to Wharton School of Finance after getting my BBA at Texas, but I decided I needed to go to work as soon as I finished my two years of active duty in the United States Army.

Things I learned at Infantry School and the company officers course at Fort Benning were more fun and more interesting than the total four years at The University of Texas at Austin.

At Fort Lee, VA, I spent many hours riding horseback, checking out nearby Civil War battlefields, and immersing myself reading the classics of Douglas Southall Freeman, especially his *R. E. Lee*, which tells of Lee's leadership of the Army of Northern Virginia. These books helped me decide to transfer from Quartermaster School at Fort Lee to Infantry at Fort Benning and my request was accepted, especially since "the Korean Conflict" was still a very hot war.

I was ordered to Infantry School at Fort Benning, GA,

where I took the six-month company officers course on managing the terrible but still sometimes necessary business of war, which General William Tecumseh Sherman defined in three short words: "War is hell."

Looking back, I posit that we are making small but appreciable progress eliminating war when "swords shall be beaten into ploughshares," as set forth by Micah the prophet. Meanwhile, our United States must sometimes accept the role of resident policeman in today's world.

(Here are concepts I learned from Infantry School and set forth as aphorisms.)

(1) *Take the Offensive to Win*

This overriding principle of warfare is that you must take the offensive to win. You cannot win a battle or a war, play sports, or any endeavor by only responding with a defense.

There have been numerous efforts throughout history to construct some form of an "impregnable" defense that will withstand all invaders. None were ultimately successful. The Maginot line of France and the Great Wall of China are classic examples. Defense alone *never* wins.

(2) *If You Finally Must, Carefully and With a Plan, Fire and Fall Back*

There are times in war when perforce of circumstances it is expedient to "fire and fall back", and as it may be essential for civilians to take up a better position or to "fire and fall back." These days individually we may face a bad (but no longer so terrifying) disease like cancer. We may gain months or even years of life if we have the will and courage to "fire and fall back," especially with cancer which more than one in five of us will ultimately face, and probably die from.

In war the enemy may have superior numbers to hurl at us as did the Chinese in North Korea in the '50s. (For them, life was/is cheap.) What then?

(3) Be Ready to Use the FPL (to Decimate Your Invader), But Only if You Must.

"What is the FPL?" you ask.

It is short for "final protective line" which Infantry officers *must* continuously plan for but hopefully only take up for a short time. Rifles, automatic rifles; indeed, all weaponry, especially machine guns, are paired so that all weapons of the command take up FPL, continuously firing down a single pre-planned but narrow lane. Each FPL overlaps with another so that lines of fire intersect but three to five feet above ground level. This is almost certain to stop or kill any man or horde of men trying to cross the bands of fire.

I know. It's not pretty to think about, and it is terrible. But think of it as your "Sunday Punch" in boxing, if you prefer. Final Protective Fires were effective decimating invading Chinese hordes in Korea as long as the ammunition lasted and the gun barrels did not melt, though I was not there.

(4) Counterattack

Remember that the easiest time to <u>resume the offensive</u> is <u>immediately</u>. If you've been forced off a hill or to fire and fall back, regroup and then *<u>counterattack</u>*!

(5) *A Good General Always Has Enough Troops*

Substitute for "general" whatever rank you find yourself in life: colonel, major, lieutenant, sergeant, or private. Whatever your rank, a good soldier always has enough troops. In civilian life this aphorism echoes with an older admonition: "Go with what you've got." Don't we often find ourselves lacking in time, in money, in education, in intellect, in psychological energy, or some other category?

It is more than incidental to pray for adequacy of resources. In my experience prayer is efficacious. The next time you're inclined to bemoan your scant resources, remember that you're the general in command of yourself and a good soldier <u>always</u> has enough troops! Go with what you've got is a splendid corollary.

(6) *Never Take a Weak Front*

In almost any profession or line of work, there is some "unforgivable sin," some no-no that is absolute. Violate it, and you're fired; your career is terminated.

The chemical manufacturing business, my life's work, is somewhat dangerous and requires attention 24 hours a day, 365 days a year. Its standards are high, but its fatality rate is quite low, lower than that of cab drivers.

Taking a weak front in war is like taking the bait of a trap, a weak front being the pretended front line of the enemy that is made to appear thin and weak when forces engage in battle. The attacking party, on meeting little resistance, foolishly pours through the hole; that is, takes the weak front. Thereupon the attacking party discovers the real force of the enemy is further back or higher up, strong and well positioned to mow you down. By then it's too late to regroup. If you've taken the bait of a weak front, you may well be decimated.

(7) *Shift Operators, (The Equivalent of Guard Duty) Must Never Sleep On Duty*

For a shift operator, sleeping on duty   even dozing, napping or drifting off   is an unforgivable sin, at least at Texmark Chemicals.   Only once have I come upon a snoozing operator.   That was several years ago on the graveyard shift, and I fired him then and there.

In the Navy the unforgivable mistake is for a captain to run his ship aground.

In battle the counterpart to this is for a general to take a weak front.   "What," you ask, "is a weak front, and how might one take it?"

I learned of one exception to this rule when I had occasion at Infantry School to meet a major general who had lived to tell about taking a weak front in the Second World War.   He was demoted to colonel instead of being discharged, but ultimately his high rank of general was restored.

The Mexican army used to have or perhaps has a dishonorable discharge ceremony in which the person to be dishonored stands alone at attention before the rest of his fellow soldiers standing in formation.   The band and buglers play a dirge while the company commander rips the medals and buttons off the poor guy's coat.   Then as an optional parting gesture the commander insults the man, slaps him, and spits in his face.

What is the equivalent of taking a weak front in your

line of work? My wife, a teacher for sixty years, tells me the "unforgiveable sin" is to walk out and leave her classroom of kids unattended.

Whatever your line of work, do not doze or sleep when on the job.

(8) If the General Listens Mainly to the Quartermaster, the Army Will Never Maneuver

To this I would add "it may not even get out of the barracks." This aphorism is a warning not to heed the voices of caution <u>too</u> <u>much</u>. Note that it doesn't say that you should never listen to your quartermaster, who in the army is caretaker of supplies, food, and clothing. It says don't listen to his voice of caution exclusively or even mainly. Risk is implicit to most civilian occupations, much as in the military or in war.

In civilian endeavors there are numerous professionals and consultants whose ways of looking at things are valid, but only to a certain extent. Your attorney, your banker, indeed most consultants, are so earnest about their specialties that they may do whatever it takes to compel you to see things from their perspective.

Don't let that happen.

(9) Have a Primary and a Secondary Objective

Infantry School doctrine of the 1950s said that in battle you should have one clearly defined primary objective, understood by all persons in the unit. In the terrific pressure and confusion of battle, hopefully you will know what hill or town you plan to take as your <u>primary</u> objective.

What about after that?

It was stressed as important to remember that a possible secondary objective was just that, _secondary_ and not to be taken on or considered <u>unless</u> <u>and</u> <u>until</u> the commander deems it opportune, pursuant only after gaining the primary objective with certainty. Even to this day I try to decide my primary and secondary objectives for the day and usually write them on my day sheet.

(10) *Clean the Lint off the Helix*

"What in the world is the helix?" I hear someone ask. "And what trouble is a little lint?"

This one is not an infantry aphorism but a throwback to the less than happy year I spent in the Quartermaster Corps. In your household you may regard laundry as women's work or not even know how to work a washing machine.

The point of this aphorism is that little details may be of high importance, with large, possibly secondary consequences if overlooked.

The helix is a little screen on the dryer that catches the lint and frequently has to be cleaned off. I tell you this in case you too are antique enough to remember drying laundry by sunlight. At Fort Lee, Virginia in 1953, I found that doing laundry was one of our jobs in the Quartermaster Corps. Moreover, I found that even though we were newly minted lieutenants at headquarters for the Quartermaster Corps, we had to get our own uniforms laundered and had to go off post to do it.

(Funny, I thought.)

I came up with a great idea during my first week at Fort

Lee! I ran an ad in the *Hopewell Times* for someone to wash our uniforms, found such a person, and made a deal with her, as well as for five of my new Army Lieutenant buddies. It was winter in those days before environmental concerns when the entire post used coal furnaces that belched soot, and lots of it. Little did I know that our contract washwoman lacked a dryer (with or without a helix). She decided to dry our uniforms naturally; that is, by sunshine.

When I got back to the BOQ (bachelor officers' quarters) I had five neatly wrapped packages of dungarees that we opened to find <u>dense patches of black soot firmly ironed into each of our uniforms</u>!

Smith was not a popular guy, and his buddies were not happy campers   correction, soldiers.

So, remember to <u>clean the lint off the helix</u>. And remember, also, that using mechanical methods to dry clothes may work better than drying them "naturally." Who knows? That lady I contracted with may have been prescient to the Environmental Movement without even knowing it!

Presumably no less than God has a "calling" just for you and just for me. At South Main Church these days we hear a good deal about "calling"; finding one's calling. Looking back at my flirt with a military calling, I was glad to have put in two years of military service, as both my brothers did before me. It was our duty. However, I never seriously considered it a "calling" or career. But consider this:

After two years in El Paso High School ROTC, I graduated as a first lieutenant.

After two years of ROTC at The University of Texas at Austin I graduated as a first lieutenant.

Then pursuant to two years active duty in the United States Army; 25 months capped by the year as exec officer of the 510th Armored Infantry Battalion, what do you think?

You guessed it — I graduated as a first lieutenant.

Wouldn't you say my calling in life may be as a first lieutenant?

But please don't tell this to anyone at South Main Baptist Church, especially if we have another one of their Discovery Weekends on "Callings."

14. Locomotives, Bells, and Collections

Back in the '60s when we lived in Dayton, Texas, Charis and I found ourselves saddled with a 75-ton diesel locomotive switch engine that I bought from Jefferson Lake Sulfur Company when they closed their Starks, Louisiana works. At the time I was something of a chemical junk man.

Now as a junk man in just about any field, you "don't get no respect." Furthermore, if you have David Smith as your baptismal name you get even less, since upon first meeting people might think it's a name of convenience, since there are near 10,000 David Smiths in the United States.

My locomotive turned out to be the first of several fun hobbies I've enjoyed over my lifetime, though it nearly broke us at a time when our family finances were fragile. I find hobbies most fascinating. They can become addictive as one hobby leads to another, and still another until you run out or space to keep them, run out of money to buy more of them, run into another interesting hobby, run out of interest, or die.

A good hobby should surely be something of an adventure, so like all adventures it entails some risk. My hobbies almost always translate "collection." I've collected a pretty good number of things including books, especially Sam Houston books, also dimes, quarters, nutcrackers,

Texiana, and elaborate contraptions including domino shufflers, but STOP!

Pardon me if I put on my Uncle Davo hat for a moment. I call this my Dutch Uncle, which I'm apt to put on with younger kinfolks.

WARNING, COLLECTORS ALL:

(1) Don't let your hobby, collection or whatever it might be damage the family budget.

(2) If you're going into collecting, pick something that has a definable, comprehensible universe   surely not bottle caps, postage stamps, foreign currency, or rocks. With collections of large numbers, you're apt to be like the cowboy who got up in the morning and tried to ride off in all directions thinking surely if he rode fast enough and hard enough, he'd get everywhere by sunset.   Had I been born a generation earlier, I might have been that cowboy.

(3) If you go into collecting something thinking it can be both hobby and business, you're probably making a mistake. A football player simply cannot run for two goals at the same time nor play for two teams in the same game.

(4) If as a kid you suffered from A.D.D. (attention deficit disorders), unless you're cured, watch out! You're headed for trouble. I'm warning myself when I say this.

I never intended to collect locomotives, though for almost a year I had two of them. Since it takes two of anything to start a collection, please understand that I owned only one locomotive, never two. Let's agree on the stipulation that I had half a locomotive collection. I'll plead guilty to this lesser offense. The advantage of collecting locomotives is that risk of theft is low. In contrast to books, there's little chance with a locomotive that someone will borrow it one day and fail to return it.

Looking back to the 1960s it might be better expressed that instead of a midlife crisis, I had an infatuation with a huge, crude, ugly, loathsome, overweight, inanimate, iron, seventy-five ton diesel locomotive. Here's how it all happened.

One day in the spring of 1964 I arrived in Starks, Louisiana to buy the Jefferson Lake Sulfur Company's low-grade sulfur remnants, billing myself as a "Buyer and Broker of Chemical Materials." Their agent, Mr. Thibodaux, was a Cajun gentleman, and we became friends quickly on a first-name basis. He called me Smeety, and I called him Tibby, but we were at an impasse on the value of his junk sulfur. As I headed for the door he stopped me, almost as an afterthought.

"Smeety," he said, "you like to buy a locomotive? I got one I sell you real cheep," adding, "I make you price you cannot refuse."

Tibby had punched my hot button. In another day we were near closing, since one of my hobbies had been checking out several still extant Texas railroads in the 1960s. There is but one step in the collecting game from collecting one or two locomotives to collecting bells, since every operating locomotive must have a bell. Let me tell you what great fun I've had with locomotive bells, especially collecting large bells. Bells are another agenda.

In my single days I visited nearly all of the remaining steam lines in Texas, railroads with such grand-sounding names as "The Angelina County and Neches River Railroad," "The Moscow, Camden, and San Augustine Railroad" and grandest of them all, then still in receivership, "The Waco, Beaumont, Trinity and Sabine Railway," which had the distinction of not getting to any of the four places in its ambitious name. It didn't get to Waco, it never reached Beaumont, it came close to the Trinity River but missed, and it missed the Sabine River by fifty miles. From the receiver of the WBT&S, I was able to buy a detached locomotive bell, which started my big *bell* collection that today numbers over twenty.

My half locomotive bell collection led to a happy adjunct hobby that started when my folks visited us at our mini-farm in Dayton, Texas, and Dad saw my bell from a narrow gauge sugar mill locomotive.

"Davo, that's sure a fine looking bell," Dad remarked. "Do you think there's some way you could get me one just like it for Live Oak Ranch by Christmas?"

I had but few opportunities to express thanks to our great Dad Smith during his lifetime other than give him a tie or a pair of sox on Father's Day. His gifts to us three boys were frequent and appreciated. But here was something Dad manifestly wanted very much, and my answer was easy coming: "Sure, Dad, I'll get you a bell like this one, and it'll be my Christmas present to you." It was spring at the time.

I hunted high and low for another small narrow gauge locomotive bell, like mine off the Jefferson Lake Sulfur plant switch engine. I thought it would be easily possible to find, but it didn't work out that way. There were plenty of so-called farm bells made of iron and sold from "Sears's catalogs" but they lacked a lot in sound compared to mine from bronze bell makers.

At midsummer I was getting nowhere. Then a question popped into my mind one day, "I wonder if I might *make* a replica of my bell for Dad by Christmas?"

I located a foundryman named Skyvara who sent me to a Mr. Grimes of General Pattern Works who informed me, "Son, you can just as well make several bells as one, for you're going to have quite an investment sunk in this project before it's over."

I found a helpful consultant on metallurgy through the American Bell Association, a Vice President of Gould Pump Company who explained that I needed a high tin content bronze for a loud sustained ring on any large bell.

I had some thinking and deciding to do, and also some praying. We were coming into fall and my word was out. I could of course give Dad my original bell as a backup, but that would be as empty as kissing your sister.

Fortunately, as a chemical junk man, I had just made a handsome profit on a nickel carbonate trade at Humble Oil that could pay for casting five bells. Then I had the idea to run an ad in the *Wall Street Journal* and hopefully sell some bells to help cover the cost of one made for Dad, as suggested by Mr. Grimes.

I learned by doing, albeit slowly. In any case I concentrated on bells ahead of chemicals until the castings were made late in the fall. Then in December I did the grinding, lathing, drilling, polishing, assembling, often crudely and clumsily, but by myself. Finally and proudly I took my first finished bell to Live Oak Ranch on Christmas Eve of 1963, a bell that worked well and had a right, loud, sustained tone when Dad rang it:

C L A N G!!!!!!!!!!!!!!!!!!!!!!!!!

I can hear it now in my mind's ear. More important, Dad was supremely happy and mounted it on a cedar post and you can ring it today if you come in the side door of our house at Live Oak Ranch, near Bergheim, Texas.

* * * * *

Having half a locomotive collection for three years also led me to a man who dealt in old steam engines, a Mr. Waldo Bugbee in San Antonio. Now Mr. Bugbee bought old steam engines over the U.S., first for their large bells, but also for export into Mexico or to become scrap which was literally "the last stop on the train."

Mr. Bugbee also never became too fond of his items, locomotives or bells, as I was inclined to do. A collector trader must be detached professionally, especially when collecting animals. If your business should become a collection of pets, watch out! You're in deep trouble.

Several large bells in my collection came from Mr. Bugbee, mostly off engines of the "Louisville and Nashville Railroad." When my boys were in Boy Scouts at South Main Baptist Church, we mounted several of my locomotive bells on a structure of bridge timbers so that

Troop 27 at South Main Baptist Church could take part in a Fourth of July symphony performance at Hermann Park. In that finale of *Tchaikovsky's 1812 Overture* where cannons and church bells celebrate the liberation of Moscow, fireworks substituted for the cannons and our locomotive bells, vigorously manned by Ralph Mills' Boy Scout Troup, well expressed the spirit of freedom. It was loud and it was glorious!

* * * * *

But let's go back to that day in 1964 at Starks, La., when Tibby punched my hot button that started my half locomotive collection. To some extent I was "throwing darts at a board in a dark room." I did have moderate knowledge of Texas railroad history, just enough to be dangerous. And when Tibby invited me up in the cab and we proceeded to start that grand sounding massive diesel engine, I was excited. When Tibby showed me how to engage the massive clutch and we moved down the track, I was beyond redemption.

Without a muffler, the engine roared louder than a Sherman tank—so loud in fact that neither of us could hear the other. We went down the line maybe a mile or two, stopped, put the locomotive in reverse and backed back to the plant, the diesel roaring loud.

Two weeks later I had done more homework and located an equipment dealer who sold Jefferson Lake Sulfur Company that locomotive in the first place. It was Mr. Earl Calkins of Mustang Tractor and Equipment Company of Houston, an acquaintance who became a friend, then a mentor, also a consultant, even an angel. Mr.

Calkins offered to line up financing for me with CIT Financial in Chicago, and in that regard he was also a teacher. I was greatly flattered when he volunteered to go on my term note to buy Tibby's locomotive.

Ultimately I closed the deal with Tibby when we got together on the price for his junk sulfur. I sold it to boyhood farmer friends, the Stahmanns, in Las Cruces, New Mexico who put it around their pecan trees. Things were going fairly well in my emerging chemical junk business.

* * * * *

What I didn't know was how long it would take for me to sell the locomotive, or as Charis came to call it, "the albatross." Weeks turned into months, and soon we entered the third year of my having a locomotive "half collection." Ads in used equipment magazines produced few leads. It didn't take long for Charis to note my fascination with the locomotive had turned around 180 degrees. Soon I loathed my locomotive, and Charis liked it even less.

Because we were buying a locomotive, we could not afford a better car. When the chemical junk business was punk, I would have to look to Charis to make the monthly payments to CIT Commercial Finance (with interest north of 14%) out of her skinny teacher's salary from Elliott Elementary School. Asking Charis to make the monthly locomotive payment was becoming an embarrassing monthly ritual.

Barbershops tend to be crummy places where you do best not to eavesdrop and not to talk. I was getting my hair cut at the old YMCA Barbershop on Louisiana Street one afternoon, half dozing, when an old man sitting in the chair next to mine dropped the phrase "our business fixing railroad tracks" etc., etc., as he paid his bill.

Half asleep but also half awake, of a sudden I concluded, *I must not let this man get away!*

To the surprise of my barber, I bolted out of his chair and ran through the YMCA lobby, apron and hair clippings flying, till I caught up with the old man.

"Sir, you don't know me from Adam's housecat, but if you fix railroad tracks, could you possibly use a 75 ton diesel locomotive switch engine?" I asked earnestly. There was a pause...and a puzzled look on his face.

"I *might*," he replied indifferently. Hope surged.

Cutting through, he was a tough Aggie with William A. Smith Construction Company, and he ended up buying my locomotive for the amount I had in it ($5,000), and I could keep the bell. The Aggie was happy, I was happy, but most important of all, Charis was happy. Now we might be able to buy a more adequate car.

NUTCRACKERS

After I finally sold my locomotive but while I was still "wandering in a wilderness" of pecan trees in Dayton, Texas, I became intrigued by the variety of mechanical devices designed to crack pecans, most of them invented and manufactured in Texas and adjacent pecan growing states. A physician from Columbus, Georgia, had invented and patented a whiz-bang contraption called the inertia nutcracker, which fairly consistently delivers on the often questionable claim of most nutcracker manufacturers "ours get the halves out whole."

In the 1980s I paid a royalty of a quarter a piece to that physician to start up The Texas Native Inertia Nutcracker Manufacturing Company, Inc. in downtown Houston. A competent and committed manager, Bill White, supervised four marginally employable men for six months for me to make a modest, one-time only profit from that enterprise of $4,000.

Unfortunately, I listened to a pitch from the Albany, Texas Chamber of Commerce and moved my fragile operation out there, together with my nutcracker collection, now grown to over 400 nutcrackers. At Albany a dishonest manager sold off most of my nutcrackers collection, personally pocketing the proceeds, and then pawned my collection to antique dealers in nearby towns. It was a classic example of how absentee ownership doesn't work.

But two sheriffs, especially the one from Throckmorton County, found and arrested the dishonest manager and thief, and recovered half of my stolen collection. I surely thanked them. Today my nutcrackers are mostly boxed and stored, and the great Texas Native Inertia Nutcracker Manufacturing Company, Incorporated is marginally still in business, planning to reopen in Albany, Texas.

DOMINO SHUFFLERS

I had a young Aggie friend majoring in mechanical engineering at Texas A&M to whom I tried to "sell" the big idea of designing and building a prototype of a double action domino shuffler. I would like anyone reading this, who is a serious collector of domino shufflers, to know that I hope to find the manufacturer of the single action Canadian domino shuffler originally made in the 1920s. Our new company can be named The Elaborate Contraption and Concoction Corporation.

Even at this late date if anyone is interested in a double action domino shuffler and/or the Texas Native Inertia Nutcracker, of which I have an ample inventory, come see me.

Moses wandered in the wilderness for 40 years, which I might have done with my collection of collections.

Who knows?

Thankfully I shifted to the chemical business early.

FAITH, FAMILY, FRIENDS

15. Teacher Mysteries

My wife Charis, my only wife, is a teacher.

If perchance you, too, married a teacher, you might help me understand some of the questions and mysteries of middle school teachers, some of which I partially understand. With others I but see through a glass dimly. A few I comprehend not at all. After 40 plus years, I'm still wandering in the wilderness, and like Moses, I may have to be content just to gaze at the Promised Land from afar concerning most teacher mysteries.

Before trying to analyze them, let's start with something I am certain of concerning my teacher wife. Charis is quite good at what she does, truly excellent, having her Master's Degree and over 50 years of experience teaching most anything you care to name in middle school, especially English. Her parents, too, were full-time professional teachers.

Over the years she has taught in environments as disparate as a rough Houston minority school in Denver Harbor, parochial school, River Oaks Baptist and Kinkaid, a private, tony, upscale west Houston middle school, where some parents are likely to suffer a superiority complex. But if someone says to Charis Smith, "You're on tomorrow morning to teach grammar or English literature or what ever," if she can and chooses to, she will go and do a superb job.

The kids will attest to having learned.

She has ostensibly retired several times, but again this year she covers for some young thing who was surprised to find herself pregnant.

Lets at least analyze some teacher mysteries even if we can't solve them.

Question / Mystery No. 1: Why do teachers go into teaching in the first place?

If anyone thinks it's because of the money, they're plumb crazy, although remote towns where opportunities are few, and some out of the county, may be an exception. Teachers' salaries are punk to moderate at best, but keep improving slightly as school options increase. Our former housekeeper made more per diem than Charis did. Thankfully, paychecks have inched slightly over recent years. Still, there has to be a factor other than money that causes a person to stay in the teaching business more than a year or two, especially when the economy is strong, like in Houston usually.

In El Paso in the '60s there was a tired saying about farmers and ranchers: "You can take the boy out of the country, but you can't take the country out of the boy." We're talking about "good ol' boys" like Bubba or Jake that you wouldn't want to change even if you could. But I do proffer this about teachers. You can take the teacher out of the classroom but you can't take the teacher out of the teacher. I posit this opinion having arrived at it after years of mulling over and living with my teacher wife, Charis

Wedgeworth Smith. Teaching is demanding work that is often or nearly always frustrating, except for dedicated teachers.

So why do teachers teach and teach?

Answer: Ninety percent of middle school teachers teach for one compelling reason; it is because they love the kids.

And how is that possible?

I, don't, know.

Let's move on.

Question / Mystery No. 2: How do teachers, at least female teachers, see through the back of their heads?

It is the proverbial question, wrapped in an enigma and shrouded in mystery... or however it was that Winston Churchill so eloquently phrased it.

For me this goes back even further to the time when I was in the sixth grade at Dudley School in El Paso. A Mrs. Harvill more than once caught me involved in mischief while she faced the blackboard.

Charis can do the same thing. Facing a blackboard and without breaking stride or shouting, she might firmly order, "Stephen Wells, you get back in your seat right now," which he promptly does. Another day, facing the same blackboard, she might be diagramming how a dangling participle differs from an ablative absolute, when she *stops!*

Neither turning around nor raising her voice, she'll order, "Robert Ketchand, quit making spitballs this instant and put your slingshot on my desk, where it stays for a week." The class giggles. Robert is dumbfounded.

The Mystery persists. "Do teachers have eyes in the back of their heads?" Is this some form of extrasensory perception, or could it be that a teacher gains a sixth sense after teaching the sixth grade for so many years? I also know this "gift" grows, reaching fruition in older female teachers, especially near and after 50. Some employ this sixth sense on other adults, even their husbands, which is an unfair advantage.

Question / Mystery No. 3: More than a rhetorical question, this is an awesome mystery—how do caterpillars turn into butterflies?

One day when Charis was teaching at Kinkaid, I came home to find six mason jars full of leaves, closed with cellophane and a bunch of pupa or larva (I don't know the difference) crawling around inside. The biology teacher had convinced Charis she should become midwife to offspring orphan monarch butterflies.

For over a week she ensured that there were plenty of leaves of the right kind for the little worms to devour. Ultimately each became a black cocoon and attached to whatever it could find to form a "J." This is akin to "bearing down pains" for human mother, I suppose. The real excitement occurred after a few days when the black "J" began to open and minutes later a large orange butterfly would emerge.   **Beautiful!**

Charis would let the butterfly crawl onto her finger, and then she would take it outside where it would dry its wings before flying off into God's world. **Awesome!**

School kids and adults alike can explore this mystery of

butterflies. Years ago at our first home in Houston we had an unbelievable saturation of butterflies, millions of fully grown monarch butterflies in all the trees. What a glorious event! The life of a butterfly is but three to five weeks. It seems that annually Monarchs wing their way to some place in Southern Mexico where their display of color is so impressive that it's now a tourist attraction.

Question / Mystery No. 4: Why do teachers save toilet paper rolls?

The best answer I can give you is but a partial explanation but still does not explain. I have come to refer to this phenomenon by the code name "tissue issue."

When we were first married and Charis taught at Elliott Elementary (an old part of Houston), she saved toilet paper rolls, no questions asked, no reasons given. From time to time I would discover a cache of them in unusual places. For years I believed they must multiply in dark closets. But as our family grew so did the number of toilet paper rolls. Rarely used drawers would fill with them. Then of a sudden they would disappear. In life we have things I call "twilight issues," ones that really don't matter enough to argue about or even discuss. So, when I would discover another lode of toilet paper rolls in a hard to reach drawer, or under the sink, I didn't sweat it.

We all agree that using toilet paper is a personal, sometimes awkward business that we don't talk about in polite company. Having little knowledge of biochemical phenomena particular to females and having had no sisters in my mucho macho family growing up, I assumed in early married life that the tissue issue was one of those things in which time would deliver an adequate answer.

One morning when I caught Charis headed out to her car with a load of toilet paper rolls, I thought it the opportunity to resolve the tissue issue.

My inquiry got a short, all business, no nonsense teacher answer. "They're for the art department," to which she might have added "of course," like any sixth grader would understand that.

Knowing that Charis' teacher network would be at our house in a couple of weeks, I decided to bide my time till the day of the teachers' cookie push. When the Greater Teachers Network arrived, I cornered two art teachers and politely tried to frame an adequate question that got nothing but horse laughs; no satisfactory answer.

I'm serious. I want something better than embarrassing laughter in my face. No one likes to be a fool. Unless we're apt to step on a landmine, please, somebody tell me why teacher spouses have to save toilet paper rolls all their lives, even past normal retirement age.

Question / Mystery No. 5: Where do teachers get such unbelievable **patience**?

Over the decades, hearing teachers talk shop, it comes home that teachers have unbelievable patience, primarily with the kids but also with their parents. I'm making a very broad statement when I say that parents in higher income brackets are apt to fault the teacher rather than the child; their child, their wonderful, unique, specially gifted, extraordinarily bright child has every right to be tutored.

I recall one night during her early years teaching in Denver Harbor when Charis had a phone conversation with the father of a Hispanic boy whose older sister served quite ably as translator. The Hispanic father's response translated essentially, "Teacher, whatever this problem is with my son, just tell me what you want me to do and it shall be done." Charis told him and he did it, solving the problem. (Cultural difference: Anglo friends, let me tell you emphatically, our Hispanic fellow citizens have Gringos beaten "hands down" when it comes to family discipline and the readiness plus ability to hold young men accountable.)

Today, an affluent WASP parent with a condescending tone might say something like this: "You will have to understand, teacher, that my child has been tested psychologically, and having as he/she does such a unique combination of talent, it is important, indeed imperative, that you give my child the special time and personal attention necessary for him/her to get the straight A's he/she so manifestly deserves.

"You see, my spouse and I are both professionals and we have a history of seeing that our children have the best because we *are the best*, and of course we expect *only the best* for this child inasmuch as we are entitled to the *best* and always get the *best* of everything as... blah... blah...... blah... blah... blah."

I call variations on this theme **River Oaks** syndrome.

Back in the 20th century, my reaction would have been SPANK 'EM!

Not the kids, the parents.

If that doesn't work, run 'em out of town on a rail.

16. Family, Dutch Uncles and Shirt Tail Relatives

When you have a large extended family like I do, you get lots of uncles with the deal. Most of my uncles were respectable men   none of them saints, but all of them interesting. You might say the gender environment in which I grew up with two other male siblings was "mucho macho." Living on the border in El Paso made it even more so.

My dad was youngest of five Smith boys, all of them born in Jefferson deep East Texas, which was once a major port of entry to Texas by the Red River. When the dam broke, the town was left high and dry. Its near demise accelerated when the Texas and Pacific Railroad by-passed Jefferson, running through Marshall to the South on order from Jay Gould, whose defiant sentence, "the end of Jefferson Texas," was duly implemented.

My grandmother resolved at the start of the 20th century to raise her family some place that offered more opportunity than Jefferson, against the wishes of her husband, David Smith, for whom I'm named. For the "place of women" in the Old South at that time, she had a lot of starch in her soul. With the faith of Abraham and determination to move from Jefferson, but no plan and less funds, Grandmother Smith took all her kids down to the train station in Marshall, Texas. Hope and Clopton, now adults, had already left Jefferson, (gone West young men to

Stamford, Texas, to learn the ice and brewery business).

"Where to, Ma'am?" asked the ticket agent.

"Sir, I want to take my family as far away from Jefferson as I can get but still stay in Texas," she replied.

"Ma'am, that would be El Paso," he replied and sold her a fistful of tickets.

They boarded the train bound for the promised land of far West Texas with my Dad, maybe four and the youngest in tow. Uncle Hope, twenty-one and the oldest, and Uncle Clopton were to rejoin them, having learned the ice and brewery business at Stamford (and, I might add, gradually becoming addicted).

Meanwhile Grandfather David Smith stayed behind in Jefferson a couple of more years tending his grocery store in a slow, unhurried way. After noon dinner each day, he would stretch out on the counter for a deep snooze at which time many customers shopped. They were too courteous to disturb Mr. Smith during his 12:00 noon – 1:00 p.m. nap, so they'd plan to stop by at a less inconvenient time to pay for their larger purchases.

Grandfather Smith was good at naps, a skill that he passed on to me. Some might even say he was a bit too casual; go ahead and say it, "He was — lazy!"

Uncle Hope loved his beer and started a brewery in El Paso, but was possibly saved from worse addiction had he not learned of a new bottling franchise called Coca Cola.

Second to Uncle Hope, Smith boy #2, Uncle Clopton called "Doc," became a streetcar conductor on the El Paso Electric Railroad Company. I still have his conductor's badge No. 120 in what I call my "goo-gaw box."

Where, you might ask, would anyone get a funny name

like Clopton? As a little boy, I thought his name had to be connected with horses, which we kids knew went "clippity-clop, clippity-clop." Clopton? Didn't "Clopton" go back to the days of horse drawn wagons? If not, then where <u>did</u> the name come from?

The short answer is from Jefferson, but I'll give you the better, more interesting yet convoluted answer shortly. Bear with me.

In the 1980s I took my nuclear family to visit Jefferson, Texas, where for the first time I became acquainted with my great aunt's third cousin twice removed on my great great grandfather's side by his second marriage (got all that?). That lady was The Grand Docent(not dragon) of The Jefferson Genealogical and Historical Society and she knew all about Clopton, as I was to learn when we met this fine lady of the Old South at the Excelsior Hotel where I politely introduced myself to her.

"Ma'am, you don't know me from Adam's housecat, but I'm almost sure that with all the kinfolks my dad had when he left here 70 years ago, I'm bound to be kin to you some way." I hit the lady's hot button. "Ohhhhh," she said with rising enthusiasm, "Do tell me more."

"Well, my grandfather was a Smith and my grandmother was a Moseley, spelled with two e's, but I'm also kin to most Terrys, Singletons, DeWares, Haywoods, and Kistenmachers. At least they claimed kin rather than maybe slightly incestuous kinship, when the family left Jefferson around the start of the 20th century."

The Grand Docent was onto this like a duck on a Junebug. In a couple of minutes she was explaining how I was   correction, how she was my great aunt's third cousin twice removed on my great great grandfather's side by his second marriage . . . , or whatever the heck it was.

Thereupon, I decided there must be an easier way of referring to relatives in question than in the convoluted terms of hard-ball genealogists. So I've tried to simplify things by throwing all kinfolks beyond first cousins into one pile and calling them "shirt-tail relatives."

Back to Jefferson, after showing us the Excelsior Hotel, my shirt-tail relative showed us the second most important thing to see in Jefferson, which is the cemetery. It is huge, with over 30,000 graves. I also remember our shirt-tail relative slowly driving through acres upon acres of gravestones. I was tired, sleepy and but marginally interested in her chatter, until we came upon one huge monument with letters a Foot or more high that read:

CLOPTON

"Stop! Stop!" I told her. "That was the real name of my Uncle Doc, Clopton!" Thereupon my "resident gene-logist" gave me all the information she had on the venerable Dr. Clopton, an M.D. for whom Uncle Doc was named. He had delivered most of the babies born in Jefferson in the 19th century, maybe most in the cemetery who could afford assistance with childbirth.

Now all five Smith boys who ultimately landed in El Paso had something of an alcohol problem. Let's face it; alcohol was part of West Texas culture, the macho syndrome, and an expression of hospitality among men. Perhaps alcohol was a *hangover* from days of the Old West. (pun intended.) So using a top, middle and bottom scale, let's rank alcohol appreciation as an "addiction" on dad's side of the family.

At 5:00 p.m. most afternoons, my Dad, who was probably "least" alcoholic of the five Smith boys would open his Grand Bar, where early on I learned to mix a scotch and soda on the rocks with the best of 'em. Today that bar with its lighted sign, "BAR OPEN", that Dad enjoyed turning on is the centerpiece of Live Oak Ranch living room and amply supplied with nearly all choices of whiskey, glasses, and drinking accessories.

Uncle Gene Smith was dispatcher for a wholesale fruit outfit in El Paso. Sometimes he'd bring our family a whole stalk of bananas. He was also a man full of jokes and fun. Uncle Gene ranked at the top of the middle range of alcohol fondness drinkers, for most afternoons at 4:00 pm his car was parked at the Kern Place Tavern.

Uncle Clopton or "Doc", was a good guy, except for the fact that he was far, far too fond of alcohol. His addiction would be comparable to that of drugs and gambling today. In fact, "Doc" was so fond of alcohol that when he and Uncle Hope partnered in the soda water business, even Coca Cola,he would take proceeds from route drivers to buy whiskey; not just beer or wine occasionally, but hard 80- to 100-proof rot-gut whiskey. Sadly, Uncle Clopton was at the top of the very top of alcoholics, even OVER the top.

Literally, "he drank himself to death!"

Then there were two in-law uncles on Dad's side of the Smith families, my Uncle John Kistenmasher, who was patient and frugal, and who married dad's oldest sister, Irene. Uncle John prided himself on saving every $5 bill that came into his possession.

Uncle Goett (Charles Goetting), also an uncle-in-law, married dad's other sister, Betty Mary, who like my Grandmother Smith failed to "stay in her place." She took a lot of kidding from her brothers, not all of it good-natured, because of her involvement in the emerging women's suffrage movement and "birth control" when she was a teenager at El Paso High School. You might say Aunt Betty Mary had starch in her soul; or I'll say it, "She had *guts*." What would she think about our gender prejudice today? ("Racial prejudice" was then thought of by many as an "emerging problem.")

Betty Mary Smith/Goetting was named "Miss Suffragette" at El Paso High School, which nearly all Smiths attended.

But my favorite of all Smith uncles was Uncle Hope, who was around the middle of the top range, insofar as fondness for alcohol is concerned. He was 18 years older than dad who looked up to him as a surrogate father. Dad esteemed Uncle Hope most highly, as did other folks in early El Paso. He was a gaunt, gangling galoot of a guy, maybe six feet five inches, which was unusually tall at that time. Hope Smith had a head to match his height and a heart to match as well, which is to say he was both smart and generous. When formal education ended at the eighth grade, he went to work at a brewery in Stamford where he learned, earned and saved enough to start his own "soda water business," Magnolia Bottling Company in El Paso. Sometimes when I visit El Paso I drive by the long closed bottling plant site and remember how generous Uncle Hope was to *give away* tasteful, healthful, highly filtered water, especially to sick folks, friends, employees and hundreds of El Pasoans who wanted something better than "water", (Rio Grande River run through a strainer).

Uncle Hope was way ahead of his time in filtration and purification of drinking water for making Coca Colas. For many years he was the bottler of Coca Cola for several Far West Texas and nearby New Mexico counties.

Uncle Hope was a soft touch for any good cause involving young people, such as YMCA, FFA, 4-H Clubs… you name it. People characterized him as a "great mixer," which he was certainly with water given freely, bottled in crates, and sometimes distributed with his bottled Coca Cola. Lots of persons today consider high quality bottled drinking water an "entitlement." Uncle Hope talked loudly, partly because he was rather deaf. He did not just talk loud; he boomed!

Often during World War II he would head out to Fort Bliss, pack his Cadillac full of soldiers, and take them to a ballgame at Washington Park. There were plenty of refreshments of all kinds, certainly cokes and beer. (But, you had to be 21 to drink beer, and you'd best not lie to Hope Smith about your age.)

During the drive back to the barracks at Fort Bliss, the soldiers would be singing and Hope's Cadillac sagging, but with none of the men out of order. All were glad for a happy interlude to Army boredom, and everyone had a grand time.

In those days Uncle Hope belonged to a flock of the social clubs, mostly named after animals of the forest or jungle. He would have set a record for how many clubs one man could belong to. For openers, he was a Moose, a

Lion, an Elk, and a Goat, that I know of and he could be dumb like a *fox*. Even though he talked loud; indeed he *boomed*, he was seldom angry. But when he *was* angry and boomed, it was about as subtle as a cannonball fired across the prow of a ship.

The story is told that on the streets of El Paso a shady character approached Hope Smith and tried to sell him a pocket watch of doubtful origin.

After listening to the guy's spiel, Uncle Hope reached in his trousers, pulled out his own pocket watch and boomed, **"Don't you know I *work* this side of the street? This is my side of the street to sell watches! Now you get out of here and don't let me ever catch you sellin' watches on my side of the street!"** The man scampered off.

Uncle Hope always called me "Young Squirrel," and I liked it. As a pre-teen I formally applied to him for a job at Christmas to earn spending money. That was near the bottom of the Great Depression and the Government Garbage Collection of assorted letters that accompanied it, especially minimum wage laws. It was late afternoon and his Coca Cola route drivers were checking in when he decided to have a little fun with me.

"Young Squirrel, how much an hour do you think you're worth?" he boomed, for all his drivers to hear.

"Gee, Uncle Hope, I don't know. Whatever you think is fair," I replied.

"You've got to be worth something for me to pay you anything at all. Come on now, Young Squirrel, how much do you think you're worth, two bits an hour?" he asked. There was a ripple of laughter.

"Golly, Uncle Hope, you mean fifty cents an hour?" I

asked to a roar of laughter.

The banter and bargaining continued to the delight of all. The final figure we settled on was seventy-five cents an hour, when the minimum wage was thirty-five cents an hour.

Finally, let's talk about Dutch uncles. And what, might you ask, is a Dutch uncle?

For me a "Dutch uncle" is not necessarily a blood relative but someone more than casually interested in your personal happiness and progress in life and who is more than candid with you, always frank.

I'll be *more* specific. In economic matters, your Dutch uncle will help you analyze changes, both short- and long-term, considering both primary and secondary consequences.[1] It is probably best if your Dutch uncle is a non-relative, for the reason that family is often reluctant to tell you what you need to hear in the ups and downs of life. Because of intended kindness, their opinions may be flawed with "country honesty."

The closest thing that I have to a Dutch uncle is my own brother Paul Heermans Smith. He is my closest blood relative and, more importantly, also my best friend. He is objective and has my best interests in mind both short-term and long-term, perhaps in the tradition of Henry Hazlitt.* Paul has a Dutch middle name from our Granddad Heermans, but I, too, am proud to be one-fourth Dutch. Mine kicks out in the lower right leg, since I got one-

---

[1] It was of great interest to me when Henry Hazlitt, a writer for "Newsweek," wrote the classic <u>Economics in one Lesson</u>, and went on to be a founding member of the "Foundation for Economic Education."

quarter from Granddad Heermans.

*It was of great interest to me when Henry Hazlitt, with "Newsweek," wrote the classic <u>Economics in one Lesson,</u> and went on to be a founding member of the "Foundation for Economic Education."

"Uncle" is a positive, even agape love appellation. And you don't have to be kin to a Person to call him Uncle. In my case I love it when kids at Live Oak Ranch or South Main Baptist Church call me Unco Davo. Sometimes when family members, adults for years, cross over and call me David or Davo the first time — I wince.

We've talked too long about Uncles, but I'll leave you with one banker's aphorism regarding Dutch uncles:

Have one and be one.

17. Walking Around the Christian Faith

In contemporary culture anyone with the common sense to catch a bus probably knows something about Christianity. Those of us who are committed to it as the faith of our lives are conscious that sometimes it evokes negative reactions, such as I had when a Baptist fundamentalist leader made the blasphemous statement that God did not hear prayers of another religion. With religious freedom guaranteed by our Bill of Rights, situations of persecution for one's faith are rare in our United States. However, arguments over faith are frequent and sometimes quite unchristian, especially with hard core fundamentalists of about any stripe, Christian, Islamic, almost any faith.

Frankly I'm gunshy when it comes to talking about faith, mainly because of how I was raised. My dad taught my brothers and me that there were three things you just didn't talk about.

First was politics, which had a high risk of unmaking friends. Second was sex; no reason given. Third was religion. On that one item Dad added that he got enough religion as a little boy to last him a lifetime; end of conversation.

How unfortunate for my Dad.

Now two generations later, I'm more than open to discuss faith and have become interested enough in theology, that I'm on the board of B.H. Carroll Theological Seminary and am happy to serve as an active fundraiser director. An adjunct of B.H. Carroll at Arlington TX is the John Newport Foundation, named for John Newport, Ph.D., the late Professor of Religion at Southwestern Baptist Theological Seminary. I was so impressed with his book, **LIFE'S ULTIMATE QUESTIONS,** that I underwrote its re-publication.

Gallup polls tell us nine out of ten people have some kind of faith. But that calls to mind the old army aphorism, "Ten percent never get the word." Some adults may "never get the word" like my Uncle Hope, who never seriously considered the faith as an adult until he was over 70. My Dad late in life updated his faith from his childhood view of religion, which I'm inclined to call a kind of "hammer, anvil, ramrod" approach to faith, not attractive, even repulsive.

As an adult there are some things I enjoy sharing: Fredericksburg peaches, Blackburn jams, tickets to concerts, favorite books, Dinner Bell cookies, and, in a class by itself in earlier years, mule deer hunting in West Texas. My Christian faith upstages all of these in importance and happiness potential, so I'm inclined to share mine, in most cases by loaning books; in some cases giving copies of *Life's Ultimate Questions: A Contemporary Philosophy of Religion,* which was pivotal to my happy understanding.

It is my considered opinion that all persons who earnestly seek God will surely find Him.

One possible deterrent to exploring faith is paradox, and clearly there are many paradoxes in life. Objectively we should come at faith with all the facts, knowledge, and intellectual horsepower we can muster, with no apology and "no holds barred." This is the objective approach to faith. So we express, study and analyze faith objectively which is one aspect of theology.

Perhaps Christians have told you of times when they had an "experience" of God, which they may find difficult or even impossible to describe. We do well to realize that each person's faith is to some extent unique. For some persons their faith is so personal that they choose not even to try conveying it to another person.

I'm not enough of a philosopher to know whether this is a paradox or an irony, but it need not be a deterrent to seeking faith with resolution and initiative. If you seek faith, you are going to find it. With growing confidence you will find and begin to experience it. In all candor it may become the central element of highest importance in your life!

Faith is an adventure. Like my dad, you may have once been into it, then dropped out, but now it's time to return to it. Robert Louis Stevenson had a statement that fits the adventure of faith wonderfully here: "*It is better to travel hopefully than to arrive.*"

Does that grab you as positively as it does me? Christians that I know never think we have "arrived" in any ultimate sense, but most of us travel hopefully and confidently with a logical coherent, sound faith. Let's walk further around the Christian faith. A happy faith, indeed our faith, is often joyful. European theologian Emil Brunner wrote a marvelous book with just that title: *Our Faith*. It is more than adequate for the rough times and tragedies that all of us experience in life.

Some folks are but cultural Christians, even closet Christians, and some may have been turned off by a bad experience. Both my dad and my Uncle Hope must have been turned off by something during their formative years in Jefferson, Texas. It might have been what someone of poor judgment or bad taste said or did. It may have been exposure to what used to be called a "hot gospler" or a "Bible thumper" preacher. Exposure to a mild case of badly presented Christianity might tend to make a person immune to the genuine article.

For such a person let me suggest an idea I learned during my years selling chemicals in Pittsburgh. It was and is an experiment called just that, "The Pittsburgh Experiment." Now I know "experiments" in the chemical business are often dull, especially repetitive quality control checks. Those people in Pittsburgh who belong to "The Pittsburgh Experiment" may need a better name for their outfit than "Experiment." Maybe the Pittsburgh Program, or Pittsburgh Trial, or Pittsburgh Adventure would be better.

Whether you choose to call it an "experiment" or whatever, it's more important that you seriously <u>study</u> the Christian faith for say a period of three months, going direct to its wellspring source, the scriptures. Why not see for yourself. You may find it not only an interesting *experiment* but to your personal satisfaction, true! Ask yourself, "Was Jesus Christ who He said He was or just a lunatic?" It might take a time investment of an hour or two a week for a few months. Try it as an <u>experiment</u>, as the Pittsburgh Experiment folks suggest, and see where it leads.

If the whole Bible, (all 66 books of it) seems daunting,

first read the essence of the New Testament, starting with any of the gospels (Matthew, Mark, Luke, or John) but read one of them in its entirety. I especially like the book of John. Connecting yourself with a Bible study group will make this adventure more interesting and fun. If you discover you're part of a Bible study group you're not comfortable with, go elsewhere. There are numerous options for Bible study out there. More than dull experiment, the Christian Faith can be an adventure that is excitingly fine! You owe it to yourself to read the Bible if only to gain perspective on how events that took place centuries ago are affecting our world today, especially in the Middle East.

You might hear someone say, "I'll find faith in my own way and on my on terms. Besides, it really doesn't make any difference what you believe as long as you're sincere."

If you try that method without going to scripture, it will be like trying to learn math without numbers.

No one can deny his own experience. An individual's approach to Christian faith is at the same time unique but universal, which is another of the paradoxes that make faith fun. As a young person who spent a lot of time thinking and reading, paradoxes were at first a problem for me until I heard "The Appeal of Christianity to a Scientist," a lecture by Dr. John A. McIntyre, an Aggie physics professor. His lecture was later published as an essay in the magazine "Christianity Today."

Another aspect of Christian faith is that it is an antidote to fear. It could be you're afraid you might "step on a landmine" thinking or asking hard questions about faith.

Don't be afraid. Questions go with the adventure. "Be

not afraid" is a repeated theme in scripture. Christians of any persuasion will tell you that God calls you to love Him "with all your heart, soul, strength and *mind*." To use your mental ability to its fullest in finding God is a happy challenge to accept. Perhaps you do well to find someone to assist you in exploring scripture, even as you might engage a consultant or coach. Choose a church. Visit the pastor. Get into a Bible study group.

A heads up: if you've definitely resolved that you just won't have anything to do with God, you will not find Him.

Conversely, if you earnestly seek God, you will surely find Him. Understand that this is not just a wise saying out of an ancient book even the *Old Testament*. It is no less than a promise of God, the one and living God; you have it on God's word.

Again for emphasis, doubts and questions are more than okay. Near the end of the last century, my wife and I had the good fortune to become acquainted with an extraordinary scholar, Dr. John Newport, the late Professor Emeritus of Philosophy and Provost at Southwestern Baptist Theological Seminary in Fort Worth. While I am no intellectual heavyweight, I do have above average curiosity, and I had the interesting experience of reading and reprinting Dr. Newport's epic book, *Life's Ultimate Questions: A Contemporary Philosophy of Religion*. Second only to the Bible itself, and alongside Emil Brunner's *Our Faith*, Newport's book impacted my faith adventure. While I never went to seminary, that book provided me an introductory course in the philosophy of religion. Dr. Newport examines questions in his book that many of us don't otherwise consider.

What would you think of a professor whose grand opus textbook so impressed his students that years after his death, 200 ex-students gathered for a symposium focused around chapters in his book? The book is not one that you will read before breakfast in the morning. It deserves prime time. The Newport Foundation can be reached on the Internet at www.newportfoundation.com if you're interested in purchasing Dr. Newport's grand opus on philosophy of religion, *Life's Ultimate Questions*, or any of his other books.

If you decide to be a Christian, you won't regret it. Faith is an adventure with Jesus Christ, in response to his invitation to follow Him, to learn of Him, to enjoy Him, and even to "agape" Him. There is no word in the English language quite adequate to the Greek word "agape." Love has three seriously different meanings.

As you study scripture, keep in mind God's ongoing offer to be with you specifically through the rest of this life and into the next. Jesus Christ might have been off his rocker to have claimed to be God. He offers you faith. You are the one who must decide whether or not you want to accept it, meaning Jesus Christ; and if you are truly open to accept it.

But if you're open to the possibility of God and if you choose to seek Him earnestly with all your heart, soul, strength, and mind, then you will surely find Him. That's not anyone's offhand opinion; that's God's promise!

18. Men's Luncheon

Men of the Smith clan, especially descendants of Forrest Moseley Smith, have a legacy that is such a fine yearly event that I hope it will continue indefinitely. It is called "Men's Luncheon." Dad Smith started Men's Luncheon in the late '60s at the Argyle Club in San Antonio, of which he was a near founding member. Some will say it is one of the last vestiges of male chauvinism, which may be so, but you need to know the family women have a Ladies Luncheon at the San Antonio Country Club. They have their fun at the same time we have ours.

Though it started with just the three Smith boys and Dad, the clan of Men's Luncheon now gathers before noon on the veranda at the Argyle for a social hour which sometimes takes close to two hours. If there were an objective ASTM test for measuring fellowship or male bonding, Men's Luncheon would score high, even near the top.

At the behest of the host for the year end luncheon, we move inside the club where we listen to each man tell whatever news he cares to share with the group, hopefully in three to five minutes — his uppers, downers, good news, problems, announcements, humor, bad and sometimes tragic news, or whatever. When a younger Smith boy comes of age, he must "make a speech" telling of his grade in school, favorite and least favorite subjects, interests, likes and dislikes. Admission age to this August fellowship is now down to nine years old, having dropped by increments from age 15 originally.

Uncle Bim then distributes the annual copy of his "Enumeration," which is the current list of all Smith family members, male and female, tabulated by the name of each person numbered sequentially. Forrest Moseley Smith is No. 1; I am No. 4. Uncle Bim, No. 3, records the date of each person's entry into the family register. Like compound interest, the increase in family numbers is astounding. No guests are permitted, even best friends, though "engages" may be given special permission if, emphasis IF, the host and/or Uncle Bim and Uncle Davo or all Smith brothers approve.

Eventually we head into the Spanish Room and sit down to dinner. Uncle Buddy returns thanks eloquently. We then proceed to read the predictions we made the previous year before writing down our predictions for the next year on forms furnished by Paul Jr., who guards them until next year's reading.

Dinner is eaten most casually, followed finally by a scrumptious dessert, centered on chocolate. (All Smiths are addicted to chocolate.)

The banter, jokes and even pranks continue. One of the best pranks originated at the Fiji house in the fifties when canned shaving cream first appeared in drugstores. If a new member orders a grand argyle dessert topped with whipped cream, conspirators head to the kitchen, intercept the waiter and switch shaving cream for whipped cream on his dessert.

Results are hilarious.

Since family comes before company in my priorities, I occasionally include spillover benefits from Texmark at the Men's Luncheon. Even though most Smiths lack mechanical skills, the Texmark tool box Safety Award was such a winner at Texmark that some year I plan to give a Cox Hardware Safety Fifth tool chest to each man, engraved with his name and the safety reminder, **"AT BOTH WORK AND AT HOME, YOU ARE PERSONALLY RESPONSIBLE FOR SAFETY."**

Are the genes of mechanical skills dominant or recessive in Homo sapiens? Further, are they inherited through the female or male of our species? Forrest Moseley Smith IV, while still a baby in his highchair, was known to effectively pick a lock when left unattended.

Who knows? Should Forrest Moseley Smith V (whose name really should be Cinco Smith) come on the scene and manifest even half the mechanical skills of his father, joined with double dominant mechanical skills from his mom, there may be hope, indeed lots of hope for another mechanical genius!

This would be in spite of all three Smith boys of the second generation who are mechanical morons! Meanwhile those of us who are sincerely, yet respectfully but also accurately, called mechanical morons must learn to live with ineptness, indeed a deficit of mechanical skills.

Idea! Maybe one day I could include the Women's Luncheon participants in our Safety 5th awards, starting with a double dominant, exceptionally highly skilled double dominant, _female_ child of Forrest V in the Safety tool box distribution next year. I've heard that Cox's Department Store may soon have a lady's tool box, made especially for women who do not wear barbed wire next to their skin.

It's beginning to look like having Men's Luncheon end in less than four hours is about as likely as my running a four minute mile. Also, I notice each year the intensity of the conversation becomes louder and a little more garbled.

Could it be that I'm becoming a bit like Uncle Hope who would ask plaintively, "Am I getting deaf or something?"

19. Baptists and Presbyterians

As a young adult, my brother Paul once thoughtfully told me, "Davo, you need to realize that other people may not be as enthusiastic about the same things you like and may not like to read the same things you read," a fact I have come to appreciate more and more over the years. Having grown up in El Paso as a Presbyterian, I went to Vacation Bible School, learned a modicum of Scripture and as a teenager could recite the Apostle's Creed as fast as the best of 'em.

More important, as I grew older I began to understand that the items I so glibly memorized were not only true, today they bring me both confidence and happiness in my Christian odyssey.

In West Texas Presbyterians, Methodists, transplanted Episcopalians, and some Baptists went to Bloy's Camp Meeting, though most Baptists preferred attending the Paisano Encampment held near Alpine. During one of those camp meeting trips I met a young lady who tried to persuade me that I needed to "find the Lord" just as she had. I responded to her by telling her that I was a Christian raised a Presbyterian, thank you, and a member in good standing of First Presbyterian Church of El Paso.

It is my opinion that nearly everyone with the capacity to read a newspaper has probably been exposed to the Christian faith in some way or some time in his life. So when this lady at Paisano approached me with something of a hard sell, I was not impressed. Today it turns me off when people insist that another person should find the Lord the same way in which they did.

As I grow older, I appreciate more and more the meaning of our Christian faith and the truth of the Apostle's Creed. This was and is something I can bet my life on.

In our marriage Charis and I found that though each of us felt sufficiently strong and confident in our understanding of Christianity, we were both willing to attend each other's church and would consider our faith from the other person's viewpoint and denominational affiliation.

From my perspective as a sermon listening Presbyterian, I knew I could recite the Apostle's Creed with the aplomb of a cattle auctioneer, so I found no compelling reason why I should have to join the Baptist church and be re-baptized. In fact, there was one very significant hang-up as far as I was concerned. Having learned and been examined on my understanding of both the Westminster Shorter Catechism and the Apostle's Creed, I saw no reason why Charis could not give a little and become a Presbyterian.

At the time in the 1950s I was selling chlorine in south Louisiana and would sometimes stay in rooming houses along my sales route, especially out in the boonies. It happens that I struck up a friendship with an old man that gave me occasion to explain my position on Baptist versus Presbyterian beliefs, and my reluctance to become a Baptist. This gentleman listened patiently to my position that I saw no reason for having to "recommit" a promise and pledge that I had knowingly made as an adult several years back. "Why," I asked, "must we make such a big deal out of baptism by immersion?"

Frankly I was mildly irritated, not by Charis but by the responses of other people including Baptist pastors whenever I introduced this increasingly difficult question. However, I was impressed by what Dr. James S. Riley, the pastor of Second Baptist Church in Houston had to say when I told him that whether Baptists wanted to believe it or not, they were in effect saying Christian outsiders like me should repudiate our previous commitments to Jesus Christ.

"It's really just a one-way street into the Baptist church," I told him. I have found that other people have experienced the same rebuffs I faced. One older Christian at the rooming house in Westlake, Louisiana assured me that theologically Presbyterians and Baptists differed very little, but on baptism the Baptists were adamant.

"Why then can't you Baptists give a little?" I would ask. From my perspective you're asking me to do the same thing my brothers did when they leaned on me to join Phi Gamma Delta fraternity just because they did.

"You'll understand, brother Davo, once you are initiated," they told me.

However, I'll never forget my initiation into Phi Gamma Delta and how I went through all the jibber-jabber and nonsense while carrying candles and marching around a room blindfolded.

Finally Charis and I worked through the issue of my becoming a Baptist. I came to the conclusion that I would not have as much to lose as she would because she was so much more knowledgeable of Scripture and active in her

Baptist brand of faith than mine ever meant to me at the time.

So I swallowed hard and agreed to become a Baptist on *their* terms. At least I didn't have to go through hell week again. I could stand up and say the Apostle's Creed. So under protest, I submitted to re-baptism in the Baptist way by Dr. Riley at Second Baptist Church of Houston, and again a third time at First Baptist of Galena Park, perhaps for good measure.

Likely out there someplace there are Baptists re-baptized numerous times, too. In El Paso days one told me she liked it "cause it's just like you're floating on air."

In time I came to acknowledge a very positive aspect about Baptists. They ostensibly have no creeds. If having no creeds is a part of Baptist thinking, good for the Baptists!

These days I am far happier, whatever kind of Baptist I am, than I ever was as a sermon listening Presbyterian. I submit that with the concept of the autonomy of each believer, there are probably almost as many *kinds* of Baptists as there are Baptists. Unfortunately both Baptists and Presbyterians argue, you might say theologically, even fight with their own "brethren" in most *un-Christian* ways.

It would be my wish that Baptists could fully and sincerely accept the authenticity of another person's experience of God, whatever it may have been and however it may change over time.

An eminent theologian Dr. W. E. Hall is an ethicist who has accomplished great good suggesting that we recognize, respect and affirm the uniqueness of others' experiences of God.

Dr. R. J. Williams, former director of the Biochemical Institute at University of Texas and son of an India Indian foreign missionary many years ago authored a book, *Biochemical/Individuality*, which describes anatomical and physiological variations related to their individual responses to the environment.

Let us joyfully affirm our commonalities.

We really don't need a great many more kinds of Baptists, but if we must, I intend to be a more creedal Baptist, without *having* to say one; i.e., a creed.

CHEMICAL BUSINESS

20. A Blind Hog Finds an Acorn

When I moved to Houston in the late '50s, I made friendships, many of which are still strong. The petrochemical business was the main driver of Texas' economy when four of us: a chemist, a chemical engineer, a chemical patent attorney, and me, a chemical trader (some would say a chemical junkman), who met through First Presbyterian Church and became suitemates.

The chemical patent attorney and chemical engineer both had good jobs and steady paychecks from big companies. The chemist and I were struggling to start new businesses. First was Arnold Williams, who was both son and nephew of renowned chemists that had grown up talking chemistry over the breakfast table the way most kids talk sports. Arnold was a new friend, even a mentor who had just started a contract laboratory business built around the emerging science of gas chromatography.

My first efforts in the chemical industry were selling dry ice (solid carbon dioxide) and chlorine gas to small town water works, both efforts were unsuccessful. I depleted my savings and exhausted the credit line of $6,000 from Dad Smith in San Antonio. I was essentially broke; not bankrupt you understand, just broke like a car out of gas trying to run on fumes.

During this time I came to realize that there was a market for chemicals not meeting usual industry specifications that were occasionally surplus to the needs of big companies. Also, there were times in Texas when the railroads had salvage chemicals that needed to be sold off or otherwise disposed of.

My first deal was with Southern Pacific Railroad which had five flatcars of water-damaged soda ash parked in Beaumont that needed to be moved. When my efforts to sell the stuff to a Houston soap maker didn't work out, the railroad offered to pay me $500 to make it go away. I found a rancher North of Beaumont who agreed to dig a deep grave to bury the soda ash if I would be the funeral director. The railroad would pay the truck freight for the funeral cortège of dump trucks I hired to carry the stuff off. We buried the soda ash, I got paid, and with a little cash in my blue jeans I was in business for a while longer.

I well remember how my suitemates, especially Arnold,

helped as I "wandered in the wilderness" trying to make a living buying and selling surplus or off spec chemicals. I had three sources of information: Arnold, the *Condensed Chemical Dictionary*, and a chemistry instructor who taught at University of Houston, who had just gone broke with a novel petrochemical process.

I was especially grateful to Arnold when I couldn't come up with my part of the rent. He would just "put it on the cuff" until I made another chemical trade that enabled me to pay my part of the four-way rent.

To promote sales, I tried several business names, among them:

David Smith, Tertiary Chemical Supplier.

also

David Smith, Trader in Petrochemical Materials.

Also: David M. Smith, Petrochemical Wastes, Residues, Slop Streams, and Still Bottoms. This was probably my best business name, though "Chemical Junkman" might have been a more accurate title for my quite legitimate business, which was to buy cheap on the buy side of trading.

Calling on Texas and Louisiana chemical plants during that first year, I recall a funny comment the Firestone Plant Manager near Orange made when I clumsily described what I was trying to do. His name was Mr. Stuart Olive.

Sensing my ineptness and technical shallowness, he tried me out with a question or two to check my knowledge of chemistry.

"Smith, do you know the difference between an aromatic and an olefin?"

There was a brief pause. "No sir, I guess not," I replied.

There was another pause; for me, an embarrassing silence. Puzzled, he scratched his head and said, "Well Smith, I suppose that even a blind hog finds an acorn once in a while."

We both laughed. It brought home how little chemistry I knew, limited to El Paso High School from a great teacher, Mrs. Lelia Oliver. But besides a chemistry teacher, I needed a partner or a banker, and fortunately, Arnold's mom, an astute businesswoman, met my needs perfectly. Essentially on a handshake, she agreed to put up the money for me to buy spot inventories, with both of us splitting the risk, and then splitting the profit, if any, from whenever I was able to net a profit on surplus chemicals. I would buy these chemical inventories at about 20 percent of the lowest value listed in the *Oil Paint and Drug Reporter*, then try to sell them at as much above that as I could get.

This formula worked okay for a couple of years. Sometimes I would have a quick trick, like selling wet soda ash to a soap maker. These and various bags of pigments would accumulate at my leaky warehouse across from the M & M Building which today is home of the University of Houston Downtown. Then I was the leaky warehouse's only customer, though I surely had a distinctive address: No. 2 Main Street, Houston, Texas. (This was before the time of zip codes.)

Besides my untidiness, I made foolish mistakes in the area of *safety*. One Saturday morning I was alone at No. 2 Main Street when I tried transferring the contents of a 55-gallon drum with a gaping hole into a better container. (Bad move. One shouldn't work alone with bulk chemicals, period!) The drum I was wrestling with contained diethylene triamine, which is very *hygroscopic* stuff. That's when a big glob sloshed through the hole in the drum onto my polyester trousers, and then went to work on me!

I immediately left the No. 2 Main Street building, crossed Buffalo Bayou toward Downtown Houston to get help. Fortunately I found a physician working on a Saturday morning at the Medical Professional Building. He had a heavy Hungarian accent and a name like Grunbaum, as well as I can remember. For years I was reminded of that accident by a "battle scar" on my upper left leg when I went swimming.

Meanwhile each month I settled up with Mom Williams, as I came to call her. Sometimes I would greet her with good news! In all cases, she never complained but always encouraged me to stick with it, which I did. I learned my way around the "oilfield patch" and the emerging "petrochemical patch" as well.

One day Mom Williams gave me a happy surprise! "David, this is too good a deal for me. We need to cut my take down from 50% to say 25 percent." I accepted her offer with thanks.

Soon a day came when the helpful and astute Mom Williams said to me, "David, you're getting along well enough that you should qualify for regular bank credit," which I found I could in fact obtain. The word gracious comes to mind whenever I think of Mom Williams. She enabled me to make it through primitive, tough times so that I didn't have to go back home to family in San Antonio, psychologically "with hat in hand."

Slowly this "blind hog" was able to find not only one acorn, but several; and, I was able to incorporate my ventures in December 1961 as Chemical Exchange Company, Inc.

That same month I did something else right, but far more important. I was able to marry Charis Jeanne Wedgeworth, a smart, cute school teacher from South Louisiana teaching at Eliot Elementary School, in a rough part of Greater Houston.

Thank you Lord, thank you Mom Williams and Arnold, thank you Dr. Grunbaum or whatever your name was for treating my chemical accident near No. 2 Main Street on credit and on a Saturday. Thank you, Mr. Stuart Olive, plant manager at the Firestone plant in Orange, Texas, for talking to me like a "Dutch uncle." Thank you, many other persons, partners, friends, customers, suppliers, patient creditors and bankers who helped me during my early days in the chemical business, or call it the chemical trading business, perhaps even the chemical junk trading business. Thanks for helping this "blind hog" find not only a single acorn, but for encouraging me to go after more acorns, which taken together provided the beginnings of over fifty years in the chemical business set forth in these rambling essays.

21. Castrating a Skunk

In the 1960s I did a good business with Humble Oil Company's Baytown refinery, augmenting their supply of refuse furnace oil as a feedstock for making carbon black. That's when I learned that they had an emerging problem bringing in an oilfield in South Alabama, one so high in sulfur and so stinking sour that it would probably require some pre-processing for odor reduction before the new crude oil could be transported to storage in Mobile, whence it would be shipped to their Baytown refinery.

Initial production showed mercaptan sulfur at a level of 89 parts per million, plus lots more hydrogen sulfide, which stinks bad enough by itself. Not incidentally, mercaptan sulfur is the essence of skunk "fragrance." A few parts per million are readily discernible by your nose or mine. As I proceeded to look into Humble's crude oil sulfur problem further, it seemed to me that it might be like castrating a skunk.

Now, I had never castrated a skunk before.

I had a nodding acquaintance with the *Condensed Chemical Dictionary* that said I was dealing with some potentially pretty mean stuff. You learn in the chemical business that sulfur compounds are nearly always bad news. Hydrogen sulfide is especially stinky but also curiously yet definitely *perverse*. While you can smell it in the low parts per million range, with sustained exposure you become insensitive to it.

The chemistry of removing combined sulfur also seemed quite straightforward. You percolate the sour condensate through caustic soda and the sulfur goes to sodium sulfate. Bingo! You've solved your problem!

Maybe!

A practical PhD chemical engineer friend, Joe Frantz, helped me with the process design to remove the offensive sulfur compounds. We built a portable skid-mounted unit that would work right in the Jay Oilfield in South Alabama, where the offensive sulfur compounds originated. My fledgling company, Chemical Exchange, would buy and caustic scrub the sour crude, and use our chemical trucks to transport it safely to the Port of Mobile, and all would be well. This was to be my first entry into chemical processing; you might even call it my "initiation," even should the "skunk" spray me.

As much as some environmentalists may want to hug trees or otherwise embrace Mother Nature, she is sometimes mean. Mercaptans, even straight from the skunk and saying "naturally" with a soft lilt, mercaptan sulfur compounds are bad, bad, bad. So in my case trying to castrate this skunk even carefully meant that I ran a moderate to good risk of getting sprayed.

Knowingly, I made a deal to buy, deodorize and transport this exceptionally sour initial crude production from the Jay Field in South Alabama. Over a five-day nonstop trial period with initially six wells producing full out, I expected to make a handsome profit.

So, I moved onto the site with my semi-portable processing rig, two truck transports, four drivers, and some 50 bags of caustic soda. We launched into the operation of "Castrating THE Skunk." Initially, all went well.

The trucks were able to keep up with the oncoming production adequately, but the interim staging tanks were filling. Gradually it became obvious that our unit could not keep ahead of the odor problem. When we analyzed the sulfur levels, they were nearly three times earlier analyses and what my unit had been designed to process. Initial condensate production was both higher and far more "sour" than projected. I went into Panama City, Florida, and contracted for additional trucks and drivers.

We held our own until about 2 a.m. on day three when I had to scramble around trying to find where I could buy a couple of tons of additional bagged caustic soda. Our supply clearly was appreciably less than what we initially thought we needed.

Have you ever tried throwing darts at a board in a dark room? Well, that's about how I felt in the wee hours at the Jay Field near Brewton, Alabama on day five. By daylight things were somewhat better. Our unit was performing adequately, except the sulfur of the crude oil far exceeded projections, and we were losing ground trying to castrate our skunk. The much in evidence odor became more and more pungent. But, all of us on the job were becoming insensitive to the stench of sulfides and mercaptans. Thank goodness we were far out in the country. Most country folks would assume that it was just a random skunk passing through their area, naturally or unnaturally.

By day four we had found some more badly needed caustic soda locally, and our operation of "castrating the Humble skunk" was once again proceeding satisfactorily.

Yet we could not be sure, because we were essentially de-sensitized by the foul smelling stuff. Besides that, we were quite tired physically, even worn out.

As day five dawned we were holding our own, in spite of negative surprises. We were even" in sight of the house," to use a family expression. The crusty Humble Oil drilling superintendent was a character very much like an Infantry First Sergeant who is never satisfied or content; at least this one was quiet and reasonably satisfied. The net gallons of production were substantially short, but the engineers had the data they needed.

It was time to shut down, pack up the unit, and go back home to Houston. Most of us had not changed clothes for nearly a week. Never in my life had I wanted so to bathe, put on clean clothes, eat a good meal, and sleep for a full night.

It was mid-afternoon when I watched the last of our trucks head out for Houston. I had settled up with the last of my contract truckers. Humble Oil's "first sergeant" had gauged their tanks. Instead of a handsome profit, I had a pretty big *loss*. But I had fulfilled my contract and satisfied Humble Oil, further establishing a relationship that grew in other areas to mutual benefit and profit. The original sulfur data turned out to be way lower than actual production.

Amazingly Humble Oil's geologist amended the settlement somewhat in our favor, though we still had a substantial loss. After thanking all concerned, I got in my pickup still reeking with mercaptans, hydrogen sulfide and all the other sulfur cousins that I could not smell and started the long drive back to Houston. I had "miles to go before I'd sleep" but I was satisfied; even a little, perhaps proud that I had kept my promises to Humble Oil Company.

I was ravenous when I reached Bay St. Louis, Mississippi around 5 p.m. in the afternoon. So I stopped at a nice seafood restaurant and ordered their largest fried shrimp dinner. There were just three folks in the restaurant at that hour. Halfway through my order of jumbo shrimp, the owner began to frown.

Then a customer came in, passed by me and said to the owner, "Goll...eee!! You sure must have burned something in your kitchen, Sam, but this place stinks all over."

That's when I recalled a fitting line from *John Brown's Body*: "Well sir, it's the trade, and the trade ain't no damned perfume shop."

Embarrassed to the extent of chuckling inside, I finished my shrimp, paid the bill without comment and walked out expressionless, though by the time I got to my pickup, I was laughing heartily.

Forty plus years later I can say we've sure cleaned things up in the chemical processing business, though "the trade still ain't no damned perfume shop," at least not often.

22. Disaster of July 18, 1982

What I call my "Disaster of '82" was the paradigm of my chemical business life; a disaster three ways: literally, financially, and legally. But, however you look at it, I nearly went broke. I went down for the count of nine, to use a boxing analogy.

How grateful, indeed thankful, I am that ultimately I made it through.

It all started one warm night, July 18, 1982, the birthday of my then partner Peter Buenz, who lived in Baytown and managed things there. Our family was at a friend's beach house in Galveston enjoying moonlight and the Gulf breeze, when the phone rang.

I heard the frantic voice of my younger son Douglas back in Houston. "Dad, there's been an explosion at your Baytown plant! The plant's all in flames! I just saw it on TV! You'd better get up here right away!"

My older son Davo and I jumped in the car and sped north for Baytown on Highway 146. We turned on the radio and picked up the news from an on-site reporter reveling in the drama taking place.

We began to see the smoke, then the flames, as we approached Baytown.

It was big and it was bad. No less than four large feedstock tanks were on fire. When we arrived on the scene, I had something of a hard time convincing the police who had cordoned off entry at Baker Road that I was owner of the Texmark plant, which was adjacent to

Humble's Baytown plant.

Once we got inside the plant, I found the huge fires were at least quarantined and that things were coming under control. My friend and partner Peter Buenz was on the job in his fire suit with soot on his face, giving input to the firemen from Baytown and Houston. It was expedient to let the fires, confined within the tank dikes, burn out though it would take several hours.

Other mainstays of our company had arrived: Dick Wall, Gene Hamilton, Sonny Allen, Roy Gerhinger, as well as several other steadfast friends/employees.

We assembled in the open and had prayer, most importantly for the two severely burned employees of Brown and Root who had been transported to two area trauma hospitals, one to St. Mary's in Galveston; the other, Hermann Memorial in the Texas Medical Center.

It was well past midnight before things began to settle down, though the tank fires continued burning into the following morning. For the time there was nothing more for us to do but go home, leaving shift operators on duty as fire watch, literally watching the fire burn down and ultimately out.

The disaster, a physical and literal disaster, was front page headlines in the morning edition of the *Houston Post*.

Dick Wall, another partner for life, and I took immediate initiative to see all persons injured in the explosions and fires, starting with the families of the two men who suffered third degree burns over half their bodies, and who were unlikely to survive more than four days.

I met two predator lawyers plying their trade in the waiting room of St. Mary's hospital, working the families of the two dying men. My anger was manifest. This was not my first bad experience with lawyers. Without prejudice, I hate them all by my definition. Over 300 lawsuits were filed against me and my several companies in the wake of this disaster.

An unsung hero in the stress following the disaster was my great insurance agent and lifetime friend Ben Baty, who worked unsparingly alongside us. At my request, he arranged an appointment for me to meet with the Chairman of Crum and Foster, our major umbrella liability carrier. I was anxious to meet this gentleman face to face.

I remember that his name was Mr. Quinn and that he received me courteously. Our meeting went something like this:

"Sir, you don't know me at all and this is the first time I've met you, but the future of my company, Chemical Exchange Company, Inc., depends on your coverage. For years I've been paying six figure premiums to Crum and Foster for liability coverage. Tell me, sir; will the so-called umbrella coverage that your company carries on my company, hold?"

There was scarcely a pause. "Yes, son, your coverage will hold," he said, both of us making eye contact. I knew that I could count on his word, and my hope was apparent. (I love the word *hope*, the name of my Uncle Hope, and my son, Douglas Hope Smith.)

We invited all those claiming injury from the explosion, their families and attorneys or lawyers, together with representatives from Brown and Root for a meeting in my home to consider the money savings and other advantages of arbitration. The case for binding arbitration was presented by Laury Eck, an attorney and legal scholar from Christian Conciliation Service of Albuquerque, NM.[2] A growing number of lawsuits were coming in against us, the knee jerk reaction of many people whenever a problem occurs that might be someone else's fault. The family of one of the two young men who died from the accident agreed to accept binding Christian Conciliation Service, but their insurance companies turned it down.

The disaster was a sinkhole of time, wasted financial resources, anguish, energy, and other things impossible to measure. It took ten hard years for us at Chemical Exchange Company to rebuild and regain our footing in the chemical business.

One positive outcome from the disaster was that Crum and Foster's umbrella insurance protection indeed held. Their coverage was just adequate. Ben Baty said there were 467 lawsuits and 672 claims that totaled some $17 million, and my umbrella coverage was $20 million! What

---

[2] The first Christian Conciliation Service (CCS) which has since folded was established by Laurence Eck in 1980 in Albuquerque, New Mexico. In 1987, when the Association of Christian Conciliation Services (ACCS) was formed, there were twenty-five CCS chapters around the nation. Prior to the formation of the ACCS in 1987, each CCS chapter was formally affiliated with the Christian Legal Society (CLS). Subsequently the participating CCS chapters became members of the ACCS, along with the CLS, and in 1989 the ACCS national office was moved to Billings, Montana.

By 1993 both the ACCS and the CCS of Montana had taken on the name Institute for Christian Conciliation (ICC). In 1996 the ICC adopted a new ministry name, *Peacemaker Ministries*, and divided its activities into three divisions. One division retained the name "Institute for Christian Conciliation." The other two divisions are Partners in Peacemaking and Young Peacemakers.

an insurance war story!

It was manifestly a disaster physically, legally and financially.

Christian arbitration of disputes is nearly always better than lawsuits for Christians, but it can still be quite costly. It is also nearly impossible to achieve results from Christian arbitration unless both parties have agreed to it beforehand, before any legal issues have arisen. However, once a predator lawyer gets involved in a controversy and fastens his teeth into the entrails of a defendant, you can forget about Christian conciliation or arbitration.

Since the Disaster of '82, I have often thought how positive (miraculous is the word) it would be if attorneys from a few Christian denominations might get together even here in Houston, to restart a viable fellowship for Christian arbitration and conciliation. Sooner rather than later we would see a drop in lawsuits, legal costs, litigation, not to mention legal stress and other negative intangibles. In Albuquerque, New Mexico where Christian Conciliation Service was once successful, an estimated legal savings near $40 million resulted to the parties concerned.

23. Chemophobia Paranoia

(Response to Chronicle article 4)

You need to know up front that I'm in the chemical business.

For some persons, this is an immediate turnoff. Although I'm neither a chemist nor a chemical engineer, I work with these professionals daily and respect their education, what they do, and how they think. We do not live in fear of chemicals. Analogous to fire and electricity, when used properly, chemicals are a boon to civilization. Our progress both in knowledge of chemicals and safety working with them continues. Without apology, I'm proud to be a chemical salesman and a manufacturer of C-5 and higher olefins into other chemical specialties.

I'm also proud of our industry and as my companies, CXI and Texmark Chemicals, Texmark, and the chemicals and pre-polymers we produce, especially polyester resins that go into numerous products such as <u>adhesives</u>, <u>inks</u>, <u>surfboards</u>, <u>boats</u>, and some <u>vehicles</u> that benefit the lives not only of all Americans but the rest of the world, too.

For one straight week (January 16-20, 2005), I read the worst yellow journalism of mean articles against Texas' leading employers, our petrochemical industry, in a five-installment diatribe with one-inch headlines on successive front pages of the *Houston Chronicle*, all of which passed my tolerance threshold and have angered me ever since.

If you're into horses, you know that when a burr gets under your horse's saddle, ultimately the horse bucks. Well, I'm bucking.

The kind of burr I'm talking about is the ill-founded fear and hatred of chemicals embraced by a few seasonal Texans and many others. These folks might need to go back to where they came from and stay there. In the 20th century, we pretty well got rid of racial prejudice in Texas. We sure didn't need the *Houston Chronicle* or anyone else promoting new forms of prejudice. Fear and hatred run together like a pair of mean dogs chasing a third, prejudice. In this 21st century we need to be conscious of another ugly kind of prejudice, chemical prejudice. Let's recognize it and oppose it. I've invented a fitting name for this new kind of prejudice. I call it "chemophobia paranoia." Translation: fear, hatred, and prejudice toward chemicals and/or the people who make them.

While many people look on us the same way, during the last the last century we've decisively turned things around environmentally in the petrochemical business. Becoming compliant with high environmental standards was not easy, and it is not cheap. I nearly went broke becoming compliant in the chemical business during the 1980s. However, with deliberate speed we proceeded to *reduce emissions* responding to the environmental concerns that were emerging. At the same time we are all learning more to be able to act responsibly, considering primary and secondary consequences, both in the near- and long-term. This is not easy and is done at large costs that must be borne by me and other producers of chemicals, not only in Texas but throughout the United States and elsewhere.

So you can imagine how irritated I was by the article in which newspaper's reporter Dina was allowed by her editor to vent her bad opinion of our industry for five successive days on the front pages of the formerly esteemed *Houston Chronicle*.

The article was entitled, IN HARM'S WAY/A Special Report; the implication being that chemical plants poison our city and do harm. She said as much in her opening salvo which was followed by two one-inch headlines "POISON IN THE AIR THEY BREATHE." A large color picture accompanying the article showed two old men leaning on golf clubs posed on either side of a large yellow chemical plant flare. With the headlines and picture filling much of the top half of the front page, you would think the *Chronicle* was announcing a declaration of war. Of course that might have been the effect they intended or contrived, something most of us would call a smear campaign. I call it yellow journalism at its worst.

"No big deal, Smith" was a comment I heard from friends. "Newspapers do this sort of thing to build circulation. When this blows over they'll move on to something else."

I'm not so sure.

But I definitely can't just smile and let the *Chronicle* run their skunk down my alley. Loving freedom, Texas, and my chemical business as I do, I reject Irene's allegations like a foreign body, or like poison from a snake bite.

After reading the third or fourth installment of Dina's front page diatribe, IN HARM'S WAY, I went downtown and requested an audience with the editor of our formerly esteemed *Houston Chronicle*. (Where is Jesse Jones today?)

Now I did not go in anger. I tried to be pleasant. I had bathed, and I had a tie on. I was greeted by two armed policemen at the *Chronicle's* street level entrance, both pleasant, to whom I stated my request. Then I gave them my Texmark Chemical business card and waited patiently for over a full hour into the early evening.

Ultimately a man came to the entrance and invited me upstairs to his office where we exchanged pleasantries, and I again asked to see the editor. By then it was getting close to 5 p.m. The assistant promised to get back in touch with me, but nothing came of my request for an audience with the editor of our formerly esteemed *Chronicle*.

I'll make five brief points on "IN HARM'S WAY," especially since we no longer have access to the *Houston Post* that we could expect to stand up to *The Chronicle's* monopoly, irresponsibility, and consummate *chemophobia paranoia*.

Point #1: Such alarming headlines are directionally as irresponsible as shouting "Fire!" in a crowded theater.

The tacit sequitur to **harm** standing in one's **way** is that we should remove it!

Dina interviewed 60 folks in Allendale, a low-income Ship Channel subdivision. She asked them leading questions, offered to put chemical monitors at their homes and print their pictures with their comments, which was ok. Emphatically not **ok** was the headline "POISON IN THE AIR THEY BREATHE." Such is blatant promotion of chemophobia paranoia and worse. As you would expect, she found some people who were ready to blame the chemical companies for their respiratory problems.

Point #2: Dose makes the poison.

This is the first and most important lesson of toxicology. Like people, chemicals vary greatly. Most are positive in most situations if used properly. We live with a great many chemicals without even thinking about them. Most we live with, tolerating them at low levels. Determining levels that are reasonable and optimal is an ongoing study.

It is easy for the *Chronicle* to promote chemophobia paranoia when we can't see most chemicals that occur at low parts per million in the atmosphere. Today the levels of suspect chemicals are but a tiny fraction of what we lived with formerly. Chemical companies including CXI/Texmark closely monitor emissions, and we are constantly reducing risks as we as we learn more about them.

The American Council on Science and Health is a fine outfit that can help persons who suffer from chemophobia paranoia. ACHS's president is Dr. Elizabeth Whelan, an eminent toxicologist. Folks at the *Chronicle* may feel sincere, but they have a lot to learn, as perhaps we all do. The American Council on Science and Health's website (www.ACSH.org) is a good place to start.

Point #3: There are other kinds of prejudice besides racial, ethnic, and religious, such as occupational and chemical.

When I moved to Houston in the late '50s, racial prejudice was much on the minds of all of us. We were coming to grips with the fact that though slavery had ended a hundred years before, we had more to do to achieve equal opportunity and eliminate racial disrespect. Today, I am encouraged by our progress. Economists Simon and Moore confirm this in "The Decline of Racism," a chapter in *It's Getting Better All the Time*, their excellent book on the 20th century.

Point #4: Dangers from some types of prejudice especially racial and ethnic are demonstrated at the Holocaust Museum.

Pursuant to the *Chronicle* diatribe, I visited the Houston Holocaust Museum, which I recommend for everyone. A tour of the museum will open your eyes to the terrible things that can result when enough folks say nothing and do nothing to oppose purveyors of fear, hatred, and prejudice. That's what I'm trying to do in this essay, caution against petrochemical prejudice, Chemophobia Paranoia.

The German martyr Dietrich Bonhoeffer noted that lack of opposition or failure to speak out by Christians was a key factor allowing the rise of Adolf Hitler, who killed six million Jews.

Point #5: The Chronicle series "IN HARM'S WAY" was propaganda as defined by Adolf Hitler's minister of propaganda.

Heinrich Himmler was his name.

"Keep it simple. Say it often. Make it burn," was his recipe.

Like a pile-driver, the *Chronicle* article did this daily with their headlines:

**IN HARMS' WAY   DANGERS IN THE
AIR THEY BREATHE**

IN HARM'S WAY   FREEPORT

IN HARM'S WAY   MONITORING

IN HARM'S WAY   PORT NECHES

IN HARM'S WAY   BAYTOWN

"Keep it simple. Say it often. Make it burn."

The *Chronicle's* reporter used the ugly simple lie contained in that repeated phrase **"IN HARM'S WAY"** at least 16 times too often in her five-part diatribe.

Make it burn?

The *Chronicle* must have intended to convey intense burning since there's nothing cool about petrochemical plant flares that it showed with its diatribes. Twice in the January 2005 articles Dina featured photographs of these dramatic, noisy yellow but important devices. Nowhere, however, does she mention what most chemical plant flares are for.

You can call this yellow journalism if you want to because of the flares. But note that the *Chronicle* meets Heinrich Himmler's definition of propaganda: "Keep it simple, say it often, make it burn." Folks at the Houston Holocaust Museum might prefer "spin merchants" as a term, having picked up on Himmler's ideas.

That's too kind. "Chemophobia paranoia" might fit

them except that if they suffer from prejudice and proffer fear and hatred of chemicals as a disease for which they might not be held accountable. This brings me back to the flares and their consummate irony.

Someone needs to explain to the *Chronicle* editor and/or Dina that most of those flares she scores in the photographs and interviews of **"IN HARM'S WAY,"** *destroy rather than produce pollution*!

In the middle of the last century, plant off-gases, together with volumes of suspect carcinogens then not defined, were dumped into the atmosphere. The chemical industry proceeded to actively reduce possible contaminants in air and water. My production engineer tells me flares incinerate over 99 percent of potentially troublesome gases, converting most of them to innocuous water, carbon dioxide, and nitrogen. My company will spend some $1,400,000 this year and next to further improve our incineration flare system, utilizing the best technology. For this I neither brag nor apologize. I will tell you in candor we do this **NOT** solely because of EPA or other myriad government agencies.

Nor is it because some Senator Foghorn in Austin or Washington berates companies for allegedly spewing pollution they know little about.

Before God, I assure my friends, employees and fellow citizens that we are not in any significant danger that I am aware of. We are **not "In Harm's Way,"** however much the *Chronicle* and Irene might wish it so, nor however many times they repeat their Himmler mantra.

Dina's attack on my line of work reminds me of a true historical incident when Marie Antoinette, delayed in a

Paris traffic jam, ordered Napoleon's coachman to use his whip on a peasant who was pulling a cart ahead of her carriage.

"Respect the burden, ma'am, respect the burden," Napoleon insisted to impatient Marie Antoinette.

"Respect the petrochemical industry's burden, ma'am, respect the burden," the oblivious editor of the *Chronicle* should be insisting to Dina today.

24. Safety is My Responsibility

During the first half of the 20th century, we had a hard time coming to grips with safety, mostly because life itself was still so laced with dangers, many of them a hangover from frontier days. Life expectancy through most of the 19th century was short: only 47 years at the start. However, it rose to over 76 years by year 2000! As I write this, our current life expectancy according to the list by the United Nations (2005-2010) is 78.2 years overall; 75.6 years for males, and 80.4 years for females.

(http://en.wikipedia.org/wiki/List)

So-called "natural" risks and accidents were reluctantly accepted by most of us through the 20th century, though in the 19th century, they were accepted readily. In addition to fatal diseases and famines, men were involved in war, homicide, etc., wore handguns openly, and with provocation used them on one another. My Granddad Heermans twice saw men settle their differences "honorably," albeit fatally by gun duels on the streets of Tucson, Arizona early in the 20th century. Personally I aim to live to be 100 years old in June of 2032.

In El Paso where and when my generation was born, several dreaded diseases were still prevalent during the 20th century, especially tuberculosis, yellow fever, smallpox, and polio. A first response to serious illness was to notify neighbors of any contagious diseases. At one point three DANGER placards were tacked on our front door, as required by law: WHOOPING COUGH, MEASLES, and MUMPS. Buddy (Forest, Jr.), Smith boy # 1 was usually first to catch something at Dudley Grade School, and he would give it to Bim, Smith boy # 2, who would bring it home to me, Davo, Smith boy # 3 even before I had started school. I remember whooping cough and my interminable "whooping" into a trash can, provided I could make it that far. In the 1950's I was known around Kern Place in El Paso as either "that other Smith boy," or sometimes as "the *dumb* Smith boy." (Bad child psychology—but effective, that I lived to reverse it and with effort make A's.) A few friends of my generation in the 1940s are alive today, albeit with polio impairments from before Salk invented his marvelous vaccine.

I wonder if we weren't as concerned about safety in the last century for the reason that we were so busy making strides in medicine, industry, education, transportation, and at mid-century, creating highways when Ike was President. We astonished ourselves at the number of lives we saved, measured by the drop in traffic fatalities on our superb new interstate highway system built in the 50s.

Fisticuffs emerged as the norm for settling differences between gentlemen in Dad's generation early in the 20th century. When I was still a little boy, Conrad Hilton of hotel fame and a banker (not my dad) decided to have it out one morning on the streets of downtown El Paso. Part of the protocol was for friends or bystanders to hold the adversaries' coats, let them face off and then go at it till one or the other prevailed, or at least gave the other fellow a bloody nose.

Curiously, Dad Smith had my older brothers take boxing lessons from a professional prize fighter, "just in case" they should get into a fist fight. But he never made me take boxing lessons. My fate was worse — piano lessons! (See "Avalanche!")

When we look back on safety with today's standards, we're apt to fault our safety record during the 1800s when our country's railroads were being built. "Railroad Crossing, Look Out For the Cars" was a safety slogan familiar to most boys my age growing up. The consummate slogan from the era of railroading and emerging safety awareness, though right for that time, seems excessive today. That slogan born of hundreds of train wrecks and thousands of fatalities was: *Safety First.*

Walk around that phrase. Does **"Safety First"** really mean what it says today?

How do you interpret it?

In the 1800s when our nation woke up to the fact that railroad accidents were taking lives in such burgeoning numbers, we needed to overreact, even if we were late. The "Safety First" slogan was tacitly accepted by most working men as "gospel."

But what do you mean by "Safety First" today? Does it mean that safety is your first and highest priority in life?

Really? First?

Where would you rank safety among these life priorities: God, country, spouse, family, TV, money, job, company, sports, internet, alcohol, drugs, education, entertainment, reading, movies, music, eating out, hanging out, travel? The list goes on. Make your own list to see where safety comes out.

Surely petrochemical work safety has risen in my own list of life priorities. It is far more important today than I ever would have supposed prior to my "Disaster of 1982." At that time my philosophy was along the lines of General Patton's view on war: "War is hell and people get killed sometimes."

Today I say emphatically, "Not satisfactory; flippant; too casual!"

Without apology, perhaps boasting, I will tell you Safety is *high* on my own list of life's priorities, though not Number 1, nor 2, 3, or even 4. Safety is probably 6th to 7th on my priority list: God #1, Family #2, Country #3, South Main members, especially the "Geriatric Young Adults Class," #4 and my workplace fellowship at Texmark #5.

A few years back "Safety Director" was a cushy job in most refineries or chemical plants along the Gulf Coast, where big outfits would park middle managers awaiting their retirement. If hard calls had to be made or there was a "testing of horns" between safety and operations or maintenance departments, safety usually lost.

When Mike Curry came to Texmark in January 1998, he brought a professional background, indeed a philosophy of plant safety. I recognized Mike's talent and leadership skills developed at Crown Central Refinery across the Ship Channel from CXI/Texmark, and further enhanced as Assistant Chief of the largest volunteer fire department in the United States at Pasadena, Texas. I am thankful that he came to Texmark Chemical when he did.

Ralph Waldo Emerson once said something to the effect that in life we don't need so much to be preached to as we need to be reminded. Well, however one ranks safety personally as his or her priority, at Texmark we *think* safety and remind one another of safety and how to do our business with constant awareness of its importance. We also reward employees holding a five-year safety record with <u>*no lost time accidents,*</u> with gifts like a tool box, as well as a dollar per day for the current or just past calendar year with no lost time accidents.

Prayers <u>for continued safety</u> are frequently voiced at Texmark which now stands at around 25 years in 2013 without a <u>lost day</u> accident! We celebrate by giving new employees a one-time <u>no accident tool box reward</u> with an engraved plaque stating:

> TO HENRY SCHULTZ
> (or whomever)
> confirming that
> SAFETY IS MY RESPONSIBILITY
> WORK SAFELY AT HOME
> WORK SAFELY AT CXI/TEXMARK

Several years back I deliberately downsized my chemical companies from five plants to just one today, CXI/Texmark. I feel positive about how we do safety at Texmark. I especially thank my key fellow workers, Dick Wall, Dave McNiel, et al, that Smith has "got religion" on safety. Here's something that further enhanced it at Texmark.

One day I noticed a safety slogan printed on the back of a notebook that Union Pacific's switching superintendent Jim Rosas was carrying during a visit to Texmark. It said that:

SAFETY IS
MY PERSONAL RESPONSIBILTY

I wish to personally thank Union Pacific and Jim Rosas for sharing this superb slogan. It beats the tired slogan "Safety First" from the 19th century "hands down." May it be embraced not only by all the people at CXI/Texmark and Union Pacific, but by all our neighbors who work for a living and care greatly about their freedom and safety.

SAFETY IS
MY PERSONAL RESPONSIBILTY

The up-to-date motto now appears on the outside of most three-ring binders used by folks at Texmark. We will gladly furnish copies for your clipboards, if you or your company is interested in joining us.

Working Texans of Galena Park
c/o CXI/Texmark Chemicals
P.O. Box 67
Galena Park, TX 77547
Our phone is (713) 455-1206

---

25. Job Inverted; How Come Us?

In 2001 the Cato Institute in Washington, DC came out with *It's Getting Better All the Time*, a remarkable book of 100 important trends of the 20th century. Each trend is set forth in graphs or tables on one page with a short commentary on the page facing. Most of this prodigious work started with the late Dr. Julian L. Simon, eminent economist of the last century, and consummated by his protégé, Stephen Moore.

Some persons might be turned off by the title *It's Getting Better All the Time*, thinking it sounds Pollyannaish.

Don't be! These incisive economists are men of good will who share the distilled results of their lives' work. This book is most emphatically not the "dismal" science unfortunately spoken of academic economists. While you may not read this awesome economists' book before breakfast in the morning, you'll find the trends clear, interesting, and probably fascinating if you realize that economics and freedom are important and run together like sheep dogs. I found their work hopeful, encouraging, and clear.

Even if you're not optimistic and doubt that *It's Getting Better All the Time,* as we move further into this 21st century you do well to consider the trends of the 20th century addressed by Stephen Moore as they pertain to Texas especially, but also our entire United States. Make the effort, will you? The trends are overwhelmingly positive. Let me quote from the authors' introduction:

- There has been more improvement in the human condition in the past 100 years than all the previous centuries combined.
- Over the course of the 20th century almost every measure of material human welfare   ranging from health, wealth, nutrition, education, speed of transportation and communication, leisure time, gains for women, minorities and children to the proliferation of computers and the internet   has shown wondrous gains for Americans.
- The objective long-term trend of improved living standards for <u>all of humanity</u>, but particularly for those living in the <u>United States since 1900, has no precedent</u>.
- Although huge progress is yet to be achieved, human beings in most parts of the world are <u>more liberated from government tyranny than ever before</u> in history and thus freer to reach their full human potential.
- <u>Most Americans do not adequately appreciate how highly fortunate we are to live in the midst of this amazing time</u>.

Following my first reading of *It's Getting Better All the Time*, I asked myself the question I ask you here, "How come us?" Do we *deserve* this focal point in human economic history?

How is it that with perhaps six percent of the world's population <u>we enjoy a third of the world's Gross National Product</u>?

"How much medical care can we afford?" is a question all of us must ask ourselves now and again and again and again year after year.

Tragically, this is another thing pettifogging politicians and predator lawyers tell their constituents they are "entitled" to, free medical care.

Increasingly we are giving hostages to Socialized Medicine, though as still free citizens we hopefully shall turn this thing around economically, but we must take action promptly and *counterattack.* We are still in grave danger of losing freedom <u>in our lifetimes</u>!

Back to a key question, <u>How Come Us</u>? How did we come to enjoy such great freedom?

How long has it been since you missed eating for more than one day, except by choice or doctor's orders?

What happens when you get very sick? Or have a life-threatening accident? Or experience insufferable pain? I dare say someone gets you to a hospital where you see a competent physician or nurse practitioner, sooner rather than later.

Friends, employees and fellow citizens, I implore you, DO NOT embrace, much less sell out to Socialized Medicine and the pettifogging politicians and predator lawyers that pander both.

If you now qualify as a senior citizen, does it annoy you when your contemporaries agonize over news of a heart attack or their malady du jour? Hey, once you get past the initial shock of bad news medically, you realize that most of us have this thing turned around, even though many, probably most people fail to analyze where or how medical costs will be paid.

The good news coming out of M. D. Anderson, the Texas Medical Center and other sources of medical care is that we have more "arrows in our quiver" whenever friends, relatives, or we ourselves have, whether it be diabetes, cancer, heart trouble, or whatever the malady.

I remember when heart attacks or news of cancer were virtual "death sentences." As Christians we're promised eternal life, but right now our prospects for living a good longer life this side of death inproves steadily. Valve jobs on hearts occur as often as valve jobs did on old cars in the 20th century.

What awesome good fortune we have to live for in our still free United States compared with *all* two hundred plus other countries of the world.

Our medical care will continue to be in a class by itself, from the poorest of the poor to the richest, *only if we reject like a foreign body Obama's advancing goal of socialized medicine.*

Compare us with old men of the Bible, especially Job and Jonah in the "Old Testament."

I ask "*HOW, COME US*?"

If you've heard of Job or read his book in the Bible, you know it's the story of a morally good and unusually prosperous man who loses everything: possessions, flocks, family, fields, and friends. On top of all that he had to endure unimaginable suffering.

And how did he respond? What did he do to deserve such disaster and suffering?

Walk around these questions, and ask them of yourself.

Scripture tells us, "In all this Job sinned not nor charged God foolishly."

Jonah had a parallel experience when he was thrown overboard at sea and swallowed by a whale.

We Americans have a bigger but opposite dilemma than Job or Jonah could not have imagined. If we take all his troubles, pains, and afflictions and invert them, we'll have awesome prosperity, health and good fortune, longer lives, good food to eat, excellent medical care, wonderful families, and more comfort than those ancients could ever have dreamed of.

If you work for a living when you read this, your per capita income is probably several times the average of what the balance of the world just gets by on. Our condition is nearly at the other end from where Job and Jonah were when they were at their lowest point on the ash heap of life.

Please read Stephen Moore's *It's Getting Better All the Time*, and you'll appreciate that in our still free economy, most of us enjoy extraordinary prosperity if we're willing to work and not go on welfare or depend on Social Security. We have more reasons to celebrate than Job or Jonah had at the worst end of their convoluted stories.

How...... come...... us......?

I,...... don't,......know.

But we <u>can</u> be thankful; so let us be!

Doxology!

26. Tenets, Benefits, and Fun

While most of the players in the petrochemical business are large companies, very large, CXI/Texmark has the distinction of being the smallest chemical company on the Houston Ship Channel. This isn't saying much; let's say more like Athens, Texas claiming to be the biggest little town in East Texas.

ExxonMobil, which began as Humble Oil and Refining, has one huge plant located at the far end of the Houston Ship Channel, plus another huge refinery at Beaumont. Texmark, which could be classified as small in contrast, has fewer than 50 full-time employees, keeps a narrow focus, and occupies 15 acres, mostly process hardware and tanks, located near the upper end of the Houston Ship Channel at Galena Park.

At Texmark we don't even try runnin' with the big dogs, for which I neither brag nor apologize. We're in the little league chemical business. Most importantly, we don't have an olefins cracker, which is a complex assemblage of process hardware, very large even huge in both size and investment, where molecules of oil are rearranged into petrochemicals under tremendous conditions of temperature and pressure. There are perhaps over 80 olefins crackers in the United States, most legendary in Texas and Louisiana. These constitute the "wellsprings" from which the petrochemical industry flows.

For over 50 years now we've been in petrochemical

custom processing, mostly serving major companies, buying petrochemical products to which we add value. At risk of bad taste or government action I here tell you the best description of the business. Because it is so convoluted, inbred, and complex, you might say that it is "incestuous".

An appreciable number of people, even here in Houston, hate the chemical business. The editors and publishers of our formerly esteemed *Houston Chronicle* are chief among that group, but park that issue for now. I cover it in "Chemophobia Paranoia."

The chemical business is cyclical and devours capital. If you don't earn it or find it or borrow it for emerging needs, you will fall behind. "Falling behind" is the start of what we called in the infantry a retrograde action, or "fire and fall back," the start of a retreat you hope will be orderly, temporary, not a route, and not be the end.

Let me set forth a handful of tenets that I have found valid over my fifty plus years, applicable to petrochemicals, and other businesses as well at Texmark.

1. **"You cannot win on the defensive in business or any other endeavor"**

You must take the offensive, even on the defensive you <u>must</u> *counterattack.*

Pursuant to Texas' drought and Depression of the 80s, I'm fortunate and thankful to still be in business. After pruning and downsizing in the '90s, today I concentrate with one production facility—Texmark. Subject to no "medical pink slips" I don't plan to sell it nor merge it, nor its parent CXI, Chemical Exchange Industries; I hope the living trust that I have arranged will continue beyond my lifetime. In any case, at CXI/Texmark we find that less can be more; indeed it is more. Because we cannot be all things to all people.

With less than a hundred people, we know and esteem one another, and hopefully implement our Christian faith without fear of some Handicapper General, or government NKVD of AIDS, or Head Honcho for Social Homogenization might bear down on us.

2. "Aim at nothing and you always hit it."

This is a personal aphorism important to me because I have a touch of ADD and want to do too many things, and I may not have too many more years to live and/or work. If you had high school Latin, you probably know that "tenet" translates "he holds, thinks, or believes." Okay, so I hold, think, and believe these tenets. They are not conditions for employment at CXI/Texmark, but over the years, I've found them valid.

A corollary, AIM always. Be sure to aim.

3. "We try to live out our Christian faith in the world of work as well as at home."

To go down this trail very far turns into preaching, so table this one. A preacher I am not, but a Christian I try to be.

4. "Work toward "Optimal Employment" for everyone inside and outside our companies, but especially in East Houston at Galena Park."

What an ideal! At least annually I have a one-on-one

discussion with every person in our companies, a renegotiation hopefully to renew employment for a few months or maybe another year.

5. **I like the motto proposed by Union Pacific, SAFETY IS MY RESPONSIBILITY.**

See the "*Safety First*" essay on this important matter. Safety is not my highest priority. As I write this we are in close to celebrating over 25 or more years with no lost time accidents at Texmark. People in our industry will tell you this record is remarkable. It occurs not because we are smarter or more competent than others, but because our full-time employees esteem each other and won't tolerate unsafe situations nor cavalier visitors. I could say our safety record is something of a paradox since we think about it, talk about it, practice it, and pray about it frequently.

Again, Safety is probably 5th on my priority list. God #1, Family #2, Country #3, and my company and South Main church fellowships are #4. Safety 5th.

6. **"Organize projects, planning, and profit action with two, or better, at least three, ... but not over five persons."**

Most important is the <u>point man</u> plus two happily working partners, but never over five persons total. Each group meets weekly. The point man <u>sets priorities</u> and is most responsible for taking initiative and implementing profit action. The point person is somewhat like a spark plug.

7. **"Practice stewardship, but especially these three ways: health stewardship, economic stewardship, and environmental stewardship."**

I posit that these three run together like dependable, happy, and hardworking sheep dogs.

"People chemistry is more important than process chemistry." Just as you must have a process for making chemicals built around operating conditions that give the desired chemical products, so you must also have employees who work well together, which is often more difficult than many people think. Sometimes we have to accept the fact that Person A does not work well with Person B, not only on a given shift but possibly also in other combinations.

We expect all of our employees to be committed to these tenets. Some persons have remarked that we are more like a family than a business, which I consider a complement.

When we first incorporated as Chemical Exchange Company in 1961, I used to joke about our hospitalization plan. "Our plan," I would say, "is that we <u>plan</u> to pay your cab fare to Ben Taub Charity Hospital, if you get hurt on the job." Though our benefits today are quite respectable, they did not come easily nor cheaply. And, they certainly do not come about from any pontificating pettifogging politicians, or predator lawyers. Neither should the "munificent condescension" of any political party force us working citizens to pay for medical care, unless we are clearly the cause of an accident.

With no chargeable lost time accidents in 25 years, I must tell you that <u>pride lurks</u>. (Sermonette over.)

8. "Keep our voluntary medical benefits voluntary."

CXI/Texmark manages to provide an excellent hospitalization plan. It is all we can afford and is made possible only through our earnings (i.e., "profits"). It does not occur because some pettifogging politician pontificates, "I don't care what medical care costs, it's up to the government to pay for it." Pettifogging politicians and predator lawyers clearly "don't care" who has to pay for medical care as long as they get the credit, and they don't have to pay for it directly from their pocket book.

I am quoting a physician friend, Andy Jackson, here. "It's your buck and it's your body!"

Medical care economics is important always. Indeed, the battle against socialized medicine in the 21st century is as serious and potentially damaging to us as slavery was to those who lived in the 19th century. Indeed it is like Gettysburg was the decisive battle of the Civil War, related to slavery.

We need something our government can no longer give to us. However, there are reasonable answers to this dilemma provided we have the honesty, courage, and integrity not to sell out our freedom. Remember for emphasis that the United States _has_ far superior medical care to that of any other country in the world that embraces "socialized medicine", including Canada, England, and all Europe.

9. "Promote voluntary thrift and savings."

Texmark has a handsome 401k plan that offers a strong incentive to save, with the company matching up to 25% of what the individual employee contributes.

Vaughan Counts in Finance says, "If an employee fails to take advantage of CXI's thrift plan, it means one of three things:

  A).He/she flunked math in grade school,

  B). He/she doesn't plan to stay long with the company, or

  C).He/she is not leveling with their spouse concerning the compensation.

"*We actively oppose runaway* government in all sectors." Reduce it everywhere and always to the extent you, too, can.

Another CXI/Texmark aphorism is, "*No prima donnas, please*." Teamwork is a wonderful word and hopefully a constant at CXI/Texmark.

As we enjoy one another's successes the comment nearly always follows, "It was a team effort." This is always good to hear again and again. At CXI/Texmark it is as much fun as anything I know. At times I could even use the word, joy.

Then there's the Grant's Whiskey Award, each "shot" being a $50 bill with U.S. Grant's picture on it. Any supervisor can nominate a person for rendering special service or completing some especially noticeable task, inside or out of the company.

Frequently there are Ben Franklin Awards, one hundred dollars with Ben's picture on each genuine hundred dollar bill.

These awards are usually given at early Monday morning meetings or Friday following. Occasionally multiple "shots" of Grant's Whiskey Awards for notable teamwork are given. CXI/Texmark is not a democracy, and I refuse to be a "Handicapper General" who tries to make everything come out uniformly equal. If working at Texmark should go down that trail, expect things to ultimately turn out uniformly *low*.

A mostly *fun* benefit is peaches in July when our Hill Country supplier, Frank Davis, delivers superb Texas peaches to the plant. He has never let us down. Employees can take whatever their families will enjoy: a small, medium, or large basket, depending on family size. Most folks prefer a half peck basket, even if it comes in a box.

May I offer a word of caution? There can be too much of a good thing when it comes to peaches, especially when they aren't fully ripe. (Footnote: *The cattlemen's term for this phenomenon is "scouring".*)

"Jam and Jelly" benefits start up in the fall near Thanksgiving. The T.J. Blackburn Syrup Works, a family outfit in the sleepy town of Jefferson, Texas, eased into making jam when refined sugar (new technology) upstaged syrup marking art early in the last century. Some early November morning all of us can play mix and match, choosing the number of jars we want from over near a dozen flavors. There are some delightful but heavy decisions to be made, when we get on the scales, (heavy as in added pounds).

There's also our annual wellness award, a subject about which I have almost become preachy, even sometimes angry.

The short version of my sermonette is that we don't support "sick days off" at CXI/Texmark, particularly like government institutions. This curmudgeon is opposed to sickness, and won't pay people to be sick. Sorry.

Nor do we pay people to take their lives by increments smoking. We tell people, "If you smoke, don't even apply for work at Texmark".

In January, employees who have not been off sick during the previous year receive "the annual wellness award," in an amount of $365 cash, which is a buck of thanks for each working day fulfilled. Over half of our folks usually qualify.

Each year in late Spring we have the "Vaughan Counts Annual Crawfish Boil" which over 200 friends, alumni, customers, vendors, suppliers, and consultants attend.

Crawfish, you'll have to understand, are also known as "mud bugs" in Louisiana, having swum the Neches River or come over in some Cajun's boat.

Now I confess to a cultural hang-up when it comes to shrimp. It's a throwback to El Paso High School days when none of us had ever eaten a crawfish or a lobster, much less even seen a crustacean till we were given one to dissect in biology lab, reeking with formaldehyde. My assigned lab partner was a sickly sweet girl from the Old South, new to Texas, who gave me to understand that I would have to be the one to dissect "our" crawfish. It was the gentlemanly thing to do. To this day I do not eat crustaceans but put 'em in the same class as most Oriental food, including but not limited to fish heads.

Also I avoid Mexican food that might include "Tripas. (Guts.)

Oh yes, – when a person has been with the company a full year, we give them a Texmark tool box award, one for men and another for women, with a few basic tools most of us can handle well, or at least use adequately.

A plaque on the toolbox says:

WORK SAFELY AT HOME
WORK SAFELY AT TEXMARK
given to
JACK JACKSON

Friday lunch at CXI/Texmark is another fun time for all new and old employees You can invite your spouse, a customer, supplier, friend, or shirttail relative to the lunch, hopefully supplied by one of these groups: Accounting, Operations, Tech Center, Maintenance, Accounting, The Crabby Old Men (Los Viejos), or Safety/Construction crew. Periodically barbecue is on the Friday menu, so someone by pre-dawn's early light fires up Unit 5299 which, rather than some piece of chemical process hardware, is a barbecue cooker.

Wasn't it Milton Friedman, the economist, who said, "There's no such thing as a free lunch?"

Someone should tell that top level thinker he's wrong. While not everybody's invited at Texmark, there _is_ such a thing as a free lunch. It happens on Friday at high noon when we ring the biggest bell for dinner at the smallest chemical plant on the Houston Ship Channel, in East Galena Park, CXI/Texmark.

Speaking of bells, another quite costly but much fun benefit at CXI/Texmark happens when we present a person who has been with the company some ten years a made-on-site hand-crafted, solid brass, highly polished, sugar mill locomotive bell mounted on a mahogany plaque, fabricated from enhanced bell metal bronze. So while it's costly, it gives all of us, the recipient mostly, nothing but fun and/or joy: call it pure pleasure.

27. Honesty, Dishonesty, Ronesty

Most of the people you and I associate with are honest, right?

Of course!

When I go down the trail of defining honesty, especially in the workplace, I mean honest people don't tell outright lies, don't steal, and don't cheat at games or on their spouses, or in other areas of life. This is simple honesty, which we always expect from all of our employees all the time.

In the 1980s I leased trucks from a fine old man, Harry Norman. One day we got into a heavy discussion on the subject of honesty, especially relating to truckers, whose turnover tends to be high. I told Mr. Norman that I could send truckers from Texas to the West Coast with $300 or $500 or even $1,000 cash and they nearly always came back broke, usually with receipts to cover the cash I had advanced. I liked to think our truck drivers were *honest*.

Item: have you ever had a taxi driver give you a receipt and leave you to fill in the amount? I have, many, times, especially in New York City.

Is this honesty, near honesty, trust, or what?

Further, what is it on our part when we let it pass without comment to the taxi driver? Shouldn't we call the taxi driver's hand, insisting that he show honesty? Perhaps more importantly, we might insist they do their part helping make sure our (almost) free economy works.

Back to Mr. Norman and honest truck drivers. I told him that of my near 40 truck drivers whose turnover was so exceptionally high; perhaps only a third proved to be both competent <u>and</u> honest under all circumstances!

"You have some drivers who are dishonest, Dave. It's that simple," said the laconic slow-talking Mr. Norman in candor and high honesty.

Then he gave me his own definition of an honest man which I consider classic. "You can trust him with uncounted cash."

I like that, don't you?

But let's drop down a little from absolute honesty and assume that honesty vs dishonesty is not like a light switch that is either on or off.

Come to think of it, my dining room has a rheostat. While I don't advocate "situation ethics," I'll tell you that cases of less than highest honesty tends to occur with men who work a good distance away from their bosses, like truck drivers or ranch hands. This form of relative honesty or even "middle honesty" I have come to call "country honesty."

Regarding our Longview Ranch property, our Operation's Manager Bob Kautzman once told me, "Our problem with Dean is not that he lies. It's just that he tells us only what he thinks we want to hear."

This seems to me to be the pivotal qualifier for "country honesty;" people withholding or filtering select facts, even in ordinary conversation, failing to tell the *whole* truth in all instances, in utmost candor.

In a courtroom we expect that it is mandatory that one tells the truth, the <u>whole</u> truth, and *nothing but the truth,* so help us God Not to do so is perjury.

Now, if country honesty is less than complete honesty, "honesty minus" let us say, then is there such a thing as "honesty plus?"

My answer is an emphatic "yes!" And there's a word for full and complete honesty, call it honesty plus. That word is – candor. My own definition of complete or highest honesty would be truth in context with candor, or using the vernacular "letting it all hang out." From my "Oxford English Dictionary," I like "frank, open and sincere." Take your pick or come up with a definition of your own.

Ron Adair is a friend, a former employee as well as fellow church member and scout leader to my boys before his move to East Texas. Today he manages an East Texas car wash. One day he observed a large sack fall from an unknown lady's pickup truck as she drove away from the place. Ron walked over to pick up a rather full sack. It was full, not of groceries but of cash, all currency in packs of bills!

Ron undertook a great deal of aggressive detective work and located the rightful owner, or I should say "trustee" who was relieved and profoundly grateful, especially since the total tallied exactly to the amount of the evening's receipts that she had lost, $17,000 of the local school district's money pursuant to a big football game.

By example Ron defines a consummately honest man walking around on two legs: someone you can *trust with uncounted cash that's been found.* So my opinion is that honesty is not simply like the light switch that's always either on or off.

Putting this all together at Texmark, we dismiss straightaway any person who does not practice highest honesty consistently.

My opinion is that there are three degrees of honesty, each of which you can refine three ways: top, middle, or bottom. Starting at the bottom with near total dishonesty; next upward and in the middle category would be country honesty, then "honesty plus" — candor, which is highest honesty. Maybe that top third is trustworthiness with uncounted cash. Finally, at the pinnacle of honesty is a person who can be trusted with uncounted cash that's been found and at considerable effort returns it to its rightful owner. This was manifested with my friend for life, Ron Adair.

I have decided to give this phenomenon a new name. Our English language, so rich and diverse with around a million words, lacks a word for this highest form of consummate honesty.

Friends at Oxford who work full-time on definitions, wherever you may be, I have a new word at the very top of the top of the top when it comes to honesty. It is this:

Ronesty.

28. AIM

Sequestered on the north side of the Houston Ship Channel just east of Loop 610 is Galena Park, a small town of 10,000 salt-of-the-earth type working folks, surrounded by Houston. It's not just a bedroom community, it's a place to which a great many people commute to work daily, all of whom are Working Texans.

It's interesting how many in Greater Houston (five counties) don't even know where Galena Park is. Everyone seems to know the locations of Memorial Park and Hermann Park or Deer Park, but Galena Park... huh?

One thing for sure, you have to want to get to Galena Park bad enough to find it, at least the first time. And when you do, you will likely find it via Clinton Drive, which starts northeast of downtown Houston, runs roughly parallel to the Houston Ship Channel, and ends at the Washburn Tunnel. A little known but interesting and sometimes infuriating fact is that the address numbers from Houston to Galena Park on Clinton Drive sometimes reverse sequence for no logical reason. Why? Search me. So, be careful.

Over a century ago when the early Houston promoters decided to upstage Galveston by digging a ship channel 50 miles inland, most people thought they were plumb crazy. But when the promoters got down to business, they had to choose a place to dump the spoils of digging, and the tiny town of Clinton won the prize. If you ever need to know the highest point of land in Harris County for Texas Trivial

Pursuits, the answer is Galena Park, formerly the town of Clinton, at eight feet altitude.

Initially there was a small teapot refinery called the Galena Signal Oil Company that is now Texmark's plant, a then 10,000 barrels per day refinery. It is fairly certain that the Galena of Galena Park's name came from that teapot refinery. How "Park" got into the name is anyone's guess. Maybe it's pure poetry. While many of us strive to make the town cleaner and prettier, it may be a few years before it passes muster as a true "park."

You'll find the air in Galena Park is about as fresh as other parts of Harris County of Greater Houston. If we can add more trees to those our Chamber of Commerce planted, maybe Galena Park will become a great place for family outings with picnic baskets in tow. As a Working Texan of Galena Park, my hope is to convert much of our several hundred acres of the Ship Channel spoilage or frontage into a jogging, walking and hiking park with trees and flowers, possibly even a place where citizens might tend individual mini vegetable gardens. Perhaps this depends on whether you believe in poetic thinking, which all of us should do from time to time.

When you think of Galena Park, think of it as a town where everyone works, because that's true. You will know you're successful in reaching Galena Park when you see the words, GALENA PARK, WHERE EVERYONE WORKS, printed on one of the four 4-foot square signs posted along each of the four roads leading into town from Greater Houston.

"Hear, Hear!" I say "Hear, Hear!"

I did some checking as to who was responsible for

erecting the signs and learned they were the good idea of City Manager John Cooper. In former years I used to follow the Greater Houston area unemployment statistics and found that usually there was less unemployment in Galena Park than in the rest of Houston, less by one percent for most of Texas, and appreciably less than two to three percent for most of the United States.

Evidence of Galena Park's commitment to work was eminently proven when Armco Steel, once the town's largest employer, failed economically and closed the steel mill in the depression of the 1980s. It was a tough blow to all. But under the leadership of the late Alvin Baggett, our then-mayor, along with the Chamber of Commerce, Galena Park State Bank, Texmark Chemicals, and most importantly our working citizens, we all rallied to reverse that severe unemployment problem.

We did it quickly! Here's how.

An ad hoc group called the "Job Buddies" met at First Baptist Church each Saturday morning to pair up one unemployed person with one fully employed person for a commitment of five weeks. At a time when most states' unemployment was over ten percent, our stated goal was to reduce unemployment below two percent. We handed out "Job Buddy" badges for all who bought into that goal. We also furled a huge banner across Clinton Drive that proclaimed, LET'S GO TO WORK, GALENA PARK!

Thumbing our noses at welfare wimps, we concentrated on networking, utilizing adrenalin, prayer and initiative to get former steelworkers into new jobs. New businesses were started. We also rigged a large steam whistle with compressed air so that each time an unemployed "Job

Buddy" got a new job, the whole town heard about it from the blast on our locomotive whistle. This became a popular rite of celebration. And a few months later there were essentially no unemployed "JOB BUDDIES" in Galena Park.

Demographics have changed in Galena Park, and the Chamber of Commerce just dissolved, or let's say it ran out of steam. In any case a lot of folks moved elsewhere. But work ethics and commitment to work by our mostly Hispanic citizens remains strong. When Armco Steel closed in 1984, and the "Job Buddies" program emerged, it was a big success. "Working Texans" is the successor to that success with an even larger vision of generating jobs in Greater Houston via new business startups. What an opportunity we have to further enhance our commitment to work, to enterprise and to economic freedom, not only in Galena Park but throughout all East Houston. Maybe sooner rather than later we can make it a goal for all Texans to achieve these three goals for Galena Park Citizens:

A). Voluntary savings of 10 percent of all income.
B). Get financial prostitution (the lottery) and financial aids (gambling addiction), and financial whorehouses (wherever tickets are sold) out of Texas immediately by getting rid the pettifogging politicians and predator lawyers who have sold out to gambling lock, stock, and barrel.

Everyone should know that the lottery preys on the poorest, least educated of our fellow citizens and their families in our state.

> C). Further, let us reduce taxes systematically, at least 1% per year, to turn around this runaway government at all levels of taxing authority.

Work is a cornerstone of both our strong Texas economy and our American heritage. Our forefathers came to America to experience freedom and opportunity. They were emphatic on the importance of work and economic opportunity than we are. Before moving here our great-great-great grandparents scrawled GTT on their old home places for "gone to Texas".

On arrival here they got right down to work without "help" from a runaway government, state or federal, and most Texans today are still committed to that concept.

A growing number of us promote "Working Texans of Galena Park, a place where Everyone Works!" We hope to be an example for all East Houston, then maybe the rest of Texas as well.

If interested, look us up on our website.

Working Texans of Galena Park
Box 67
Galena Park, TX 77547-0067
Phone 713.455.1206

29. Depressions

During the '70s, Houston and all Texas enjoyed consistent prosperity, though with occasional downward spikes that we always knew were temporary. Both the petroleum and petrochemical industries were thriving, together with their support businesses. The Port of Houston was booming. Greater Houston's banks, some two hundred (yes, 200) of them, seemed to have more loan opportunities than they could address.

Most Texas towns had Chambers of Commerce, though business deals multiplied through innumerable social, religious, and/or other networks wherever and however business people came together, including my old Ben Milam Hotel Coffee Shop on Texas Avenue, which was the defacto meeting place in the early, early morning for Greater Houston's construction fraternity. New companies were starting up daily – D.B.As., partnerships, corporations, proprietorships, and all varieties of working Texans sought to get in on the seemingly irrepressible Houston and all Texas boom.

In my own case, trading in petrochemical by-products and chemical junk were my focus. By cutting and trying, I found a small business recipe that often worked. I would find a person enthusiastic with a new petrochemical business idea. (Then with this initiator or point man I would put a person of high technical competence, plus a financial officer of highest quality, as well as informal management emphasizing "implementing profitable action.") Albeit undercapitalized, my main outfit, Chemical Exchange, provided services and a degree of organization. I had partners, most of whom I could trust and with bankers anxious to loan out money, I was running trumps.

Soon I had eight, and then a dozen, ultimately near 20 small, petroleum and chemical-related firms, with only two to five employees. Most of the outfits were marginally profitable, two or three were quite profitable, and at least three others were money losers that we "knew" would soon get out of the red. Five were Greater Houston companies with production facilities and plant sites that seemed always to need more cash for process hardware, plus working capital. As I mentioned earlier, Greater Houston had some 200 independent banks to choose from!

What I call my Disaster of '82 occurred from a compounding of three unlikely factors that should never have happened, but did. On July 18th, 1982, an unexplained ignition source detonated a huge inventory of propylene oxide causing a fireball that "sunburned" around 30 men; two of whom died within three days of the explosion.

When the initial fires were brought under control, Peter Buenz, Dick Wall and I, along with a dozen other employees, gathered inside my then Baytown Plant for prayer.

Predator lawyers also gathered like vultures around a probably small dying animal, and once they had fastened their talons into us, our insurers, and other related parties, north of 300 lawsuits were pending against me and/or my companies.   Efforts to utilize binding arbitration by Christian Arbitration and Conciliation Services were fruitless. Thanks to most of the parties concerned, and most importantly to God, we survived. But the rest of the 1980s and '90s were extremely tough paying back debts and/or judgments to the minority of creditors who felt compelled to defer to predator lawyers who functioned as fight promoters, as many still do: "Let's you and him fight!"

In my early days growing up in El Paso, Dad was a banker and ranch loan officer at State National Bank, then the larger of the city's two banks. Tentatively hoping one day to be a businessman or maybe even a banker, I listened to all of Dad's banker aphorisms, starting with, "It's easier to borrow than to pay back." I didn't learn that one very well until my Disaster of '82 when I learned *how much* harder paying back would be than borrowing.

Another aphorism came home with force in the 1980s and '90s pursuant to the Baytown Disaster. It is: "You cannot borrow your way out of debt. You have to <u>earn</u> your way out of debt", and for me, the first step was liquidating certain precious assets.

Most distressing personally was selling my Galena Park State Bank, then thoroughly sound with 14 percent capitalization, less than 50 percent loans and a cost of funds spread of three and three quarter points. (Translate: a profitable and a conservative bank.)

It was expedient for me to sell the bank to provide liquidity for my chemical businesses and to endow a committed Music Chair promised to Southwestern Baptist Theological Seminary.

The man that I sold Galena Park State Bank to was a "go-go banker" who ran it aground in two short years.

"Don't go on others' notes," was another of Dad Smith's banker aphorisms. Technically I may not have endorsed other people's notes, but since I was the main owner of most of my companies in which "partners" had paid in little or no capital or cash, results were the same. In the early '80s, it got down to bankers asking something like, "Smith, don't you believe in the success of your enterprises? You aren't afraid to jump with your own parachute, or are you?"

When I think back to my response, the word that comes to mind is "cavalier."

Another businessman or banker's aphorism is "Try never to invade your capital." To my view this was more an ideal than an absolute, even a commandment. Following the Disaster of '82, it became necessary for me to "invade capital," I sold my bank and most of a valuable document collection of Texiana, for which I neither brag nor apologize. Isn't economic life largely a matter of changing priorities? We have needs and challenges, and hopefully we have assets and production capabilities. In fact, in any business, we are always traders. Reconciling priorities in an ever changing world is an adventure. But "adventure" is too nice a word, too happy. To me it has a storybook aspect implying that the ending will turn out nicely and the characters will live happily ever after.

There was no prospect of my not invading capital in the '80s. Business was in sharp decline and it was hard to sell dwindling assets at prices adequate to pay due and overdue liabilities. It's hard to convey how awkward it is to call on a creditor with the bad news that you can't pay him at the time, and you're not sure when you can. I resolved however to take the initiative and go around to my three-page list of creditors, many of whom I had never met personally. How would they react? I assumed with displeasure for sure. But would they be angry, even hostile?

With "hat in hand" figuratively, in December of 1985 I began to see all these creditors to reconfirm my commitment to pay at least all principal. It was essential that unilaterally I stop further interest. Otherwise, I explained, the compounding of interest would carry my debts into outer space. I implored my creditors, "Do not, please do not, force me into the unmentionable ten letter "b-word." . . . (bankruptcy). Repeatedly I would make my speech, hopefully to the person who was the decision maker, "Sir, if you will work with me and not sue me, I will not let you down. By our working together there will be more money to apply on debts instead of being thrown away on predator lawyers. I will keep you posted on my progress on at least a quarterly basis."

The fact that I spent a lot of time making such calls that might otherwise have been used generating earnings seemed wise. Rather than only seeing these creditors to update my progress, I made it a practice always to deliver some payment, even if it were just fifty bucks. In the 1980s depression, when I brought money, no one was ever "in a meeting" or too busy to see me. No one threw me out of his office.

It would be nice to say that all of the creditors listed on my three pages were positive. Some few were nonresponsive, but then one day the deputy sheriff would show up to present a formal notice of a lawsuit against me or one of my companies or contractors. Two-thirds of my creditors were financial institutions and/or banks. Sometimes a mealy mouthed hack in the organization would say in effect, "Nothing personal, Smith. We just need to be first in line legally in case your plan doesn't work and you go bankrupt. We need to file now to have a recorded legal judgment." Sometimes in court, I would appear without counsel before the judge, confirming that I owed the money but was not able to pay at that time. A steadfast friend and legal counselor always willing to put cost of services "on the cuff" was Bill Byrd. To this day I agape love the memory of Bill Byrd and his banker father-in-law Dooley Dawson. Humble, today Exxon Mobil, cut me considerable slack, for which I was and remain, grateful.

Throughout this period only seven creditors listed on the three double-spaced pages would sick their "junkyard dog lawyers" on me. Thankfully no two sued me at the same time. Under Texas law, had any two trigger happy lawyers met together to bring suit, they could have straightaway thrown me into involuntary bankruptcy.

Believing both in adrenalin and in prayer, I worked hard and prayed earnestly, hoping somehow I could prove worthy of further extended terms until I could also generate higher earnings.

30. To Work, Give and Venture in a Still Free Economy?

The years move on and the value of two, sometimes three miles jogging is confirmed day after day. Sometimes I'll jog around Galena Park, watching dawn break and the lights go off along the ship channel. Then there are mornings when rain delays things.

Sometimes we even have what we used to call in El Paso a "gully washer." That old saying "if you don't like Texas weather wait 20 minutes" might well be amended to say, "If you don't like Texas climate, drive a hundred miles." It's less than 16 miles from my house to the plant and I tell you there are times when we have a gully washer one place but it's dry as a bone at the other. I've even experienced wet and dry contrasts during the full three-mile jogs around Rice University.

As I write this, it's a glorious morning in Birmingham, AL where I just came in from a half hour jogging repeatedly around AmeriSuites where I'm staying. A busy housekeeper spoke to me when I finished jogging. "I wish I had your energy," she said, to which I responded, "I wish I had your years." We both chuckled. Next morning I nodded to this busy, happy housekeeper as I headed out for my morning run. Later that day I found one of my personal Pisano tie tacks and gave it to her. Giving a paisano pin is my way to salute or say thank you to anyone at any time for any reason.

I consider Galena Park, my business hometown, we have a word of greeting between people that is also a salute. We say "paisano," which I said, moderately. She responded, "paisano!" We chatted a bit, exchanged names, and I further explained the paisano story.

> "This bird of the Southwest can be found throughout the Chihuahuan desert especially in West Texas. He, the Paisano, was of special interest to early explorers because of his friendliness. Some persons call him "roadrunner" or consider him a clown, but I prefer the distinctive "paisano!"

> Especially out in far West Texas, I look for the paisano through sometimes we see them at Live Oak Ranch. In both Spanish, Italian, and now Texas English "paisano" is a term of rugged endearment, perhaps best translated compatriot or fellow countryman.

> The bird is down to earth and seldom flies, will take on formidable tasks, even attaching rattlesnakes. Fellow Texan Wyman Meinzer of Benjamin, Texas has written a book with photographs about the paisano.

> Sometimes he stops as though trying to tell us something . . . . . .

> Maybe it's that we too should stop sometimes to salute a person whom we esteem for the work they do, the service they render, perhaps for a fine relationship or special friendship, or just to say thank you. A friend in Roswell, New Mexico handcrafts these pins for me of silver.

And so I want to give you this pin and thank you for
the person you are, for your fine character, for the
service you render and especially for the work
you do, and a salute . . . ."

PAISANO !

"Lilly Hill," I told her, "you obviously do a good job for
these folks. How long have you been with AmeriSuites?"

"Seven years," she said with a smile.

"There are lots of people who live in Galena Park and
work for a living, so we have a group called Working
Texans who recognize proud working people. Though you
can live any place, I want to recognize you as a founding
member of "Working Texans" with this paisano pin, if you
want to have it. We aim to have a hundred active
members committed to optimal employment."

Lilly was pleased and said she would like to be part of it.

Since my conversation with Lilly I've decided to move
forward with "Working Texans of Galena Park" which will
promote Optimal Employment starting at Galena Park,
Harris County, Texas, and other counties of Greater
Houston; indeed, all 254 counties of Texas.

A few years back during vacation with lifelong friends,
Don and Mary Langford, Don and I were talking about the
future and I found out that both of us have programs for
maintaining our health and neither of us plans to retire
anytime soon. I told Don that I wanted to make a bumper
sticker for Working Texans that says *ABOLISH
RETIREMENT*.

Carrying that idea further, I asked him, "Why don't we
both aim to live to be a hundred? Since Dayton days I've

kept my daily jogging program quite consistently and you're obviously keeping up your own health at the same time you're working at your practice."

"Let's do it," Don responded, and he proceeded to draw up articles of agreement in his best but illegible physician's handwriting, and our wives witnessed our signing the single page document. We intend to hold one another accountable as well as encourage each other, which Christian friends tend to do anyway.

Corollary to setting goals for one's health is setting priorities among one's projects. Second only to my optimizing profit at Texmark will be my promoting optimal employment through *Working Texans of Galena Park*.

I can say without apology, (bragging, maybe) that we in Galena Park have been leaders in improving the atmosphere all along the Houston Ship Channel. I can also tell you that when I first acquired the Texmark plant, over 40 years ago, the atmosphere of Greater Galena Park and all Harris County had many odors and smells, some good, but most were not so good foul, stinking, polluting and repugnant.

I used to think it might be a fun game to blindfold and ask a Houstonian if he could tell where he was plus or minus a half-mile in Harris County by the smells. Among the clearly identifiable odors some 40 years ago were from the packing plants, (two of them), the carbon black plants and the smell from the Sinclair Refinery that processed the most rotten smelly sour crude, the bakery plant (an attractive smell), yes and when the wind was right, the smell of my own olefins plant in and around Galena Park. Most offensive of all whether in Galena Park or around

Rice University, would have been the Phoenix Chemical plant discharging hundreds of tons of hydrogen sulfide and sulfur dioxide some dozen miles away.

Brassy! Ugh!

That stuff was bad, noxious, toxic, carcinogenic, especially when I'd go out for the morning paper at home or for a Sunday run.

Running the TEXAS MILE (Texas Avenue is exactly 1.35 miles one way) in Downtown Houston always makes for a good jog. I especially enjoy it by dawn's early light on Sunday mornings when few people are around, especially if we have a glorious sunrise.

After jogging, I pause to look around with delight at our awesome City of Houston. I thought about its opportunity, its cultural diversity, our prosperity, and the high confidence level among most of our fellow citizens; "Oh Joy, Oh Rapture Unforeseen" (Gilbert and Sullivan).

Any way you look at Houston could be well expressed in the words of the apostle Paul. "We are citizens of no mean city."

I most emphatically and unreservedly plan to continue to live here, give here, work here, jog here and seek other business ventures here. I'm grateful to be able to live in Houston, which is my bedroom community, Galena Park, which is my working community, as well as the eight adjoining counties (Brazoria, Chambers, Fort Bend, Galveston, Harris, Liberty, Montgomery, and Waller) that comprise Greater Houston in which I roam.

31. Saddam Hussein, Adolph Hitler, You and Me

How do you explain dictators? Why are there so many of them? While Saddam Hussein may have been given summary death, we can be sure he will not go down in history as the last horrible dictator.

As a little boy I remember Adolph Hitler as someone whom the Western world really didn't want to take seriously. Both England and the United States stood back in detachment as Hitler took over all Germany's neighbors and in three short weeks the wimps of France; all the while talking peace diplomatically.

Somehow he convinced the church in Germany that his movement was a moral one but then proceeded to murder six million Jews.

And I do remember how Neville Chamberlain of Britain was quite as willing to write off the rest of Europe if Hitler would kindly promise to leave England alone. Fortunately, even providentially Churchill, with starch in his soul, courage and eloquence, rallied Britain to get involved before it was too late.

Then as now many folks sincerely believed the way to handle dictators is by thinking good, nice thoughts and wishing they'd go away.

Hitler was joined by Italy's Benito Mussolini, ostensibly a friendly man. Then Stalin came on the scene in Russia, not smiling but murdering millions in Eastern Europe which we in the United States were almost certainly aware of. With the Atlantic Ocean to the east and the Pacific Ocean to the west, America felt secure "from sea to shining sea," just like the hymn, "American the Beautiful" said.

Let's remember that we Americans are capable of fatuous wishful thinking, as manifested when we permitted and participated in a most unholy alliance at Potsdam with Stalin.

Meanwhile, dictators were emerging in the Far East, most notably Tojo and Hirohito of Japan. Few of us these days remember December 7th of 1941 as vividly as 9/11 is known today.

Now, please a discursive.

Among several interesting institutions in our Houston Museum District, there is one that I consider essential for every thinking and freedom loving Texan to peruse carefully, even prayerfully—the Holocaust Museum. Its subject matter is ugly, graphic, ghastly, evil, and repulsive, but overriding all, it is historically true. With clarity and impact it brings home just how fragile our freedom is.

Pause to consider and remember that we too can lose our freedom, quite as quickly as the German people lost theirs. The Holocaust Museum Library has on hand many copies of *A Century of Genocide* which gives accounts of over 15 mass killers besides Hitler's genocide of six million Jews. Also, you can check out these names in *Wikipedia*: Mao Zedong of China; Kim Il-Sung of North Korea; Ferdinand Marcos of the Philippines; Jean-Claude Duvalier of Haiti; Ceausescu of Romania; the list goes on and on.

* * * * *

We Americans can lose our freedom too, the Constitution and Bill of Rights, notwithstanding. Indeed, we almost lost our faith in freedom and the market economy during The Great Depression when we "legally" granted near dictatorial powers to Franklin Roosevelt on par with Germany's Weimar Republic handover to Hitler! FDR's legacy was an incomprehensible and prolix burden of laws and the overture for today's runaway government. We have underwritten a playpen in Washington, D.C. far larger than our Texas' playpen at Austin. Pettifogging politicians and predator lawyers dissipate huge portions of our Texas GNP. Then they, the pettifogging politicians in Austin and Washington, DC, stand in the attitude of benefactors, "giving" back to us though their laws, in violation of the constitution _what is NOT theirs to give_!

We passively watch and do nothing as they prattle, parade and proudly pontificate, exchanging and keeping elegant pens as mementos and keepsakes of what they proudly, albeit wrongly, consider wonderful legal handiwork.

Yes, we can lose our freedom. We are losing it. We continue to lose it by indifference, irresponsibility and default to the lawmakers, the majority of whom are lawyers in their playpens that we lesser citizens underwrite in Austin, TX and Washington, DC, as well as 49 other state capitals plus tens of thousands of government offices. There is a solution in operation by our English cousins. It is quite simply this: the loser of a lawsuit pays <u>all</u>, emphasis **ALL**, costs connected with a plaintiff's lawsuit in the UK. Walk around that prospect for us here in the United States.

Have you ever looked at the percentage of lawyers holding seats in our legislatures compared to those from other more honest trades? Each pettifogging politician, which is to say career politician who has not ever made an honest living making a product, providing a service or meeting a payroll). I would make it a requirement that no one be a "career politician" limiting each to no more than two terms or six years period

<u>NO</u> career politicians; none!.

A stipulation, please: When I use the term "predator lawyer" or merely "lawyer," please know that I do not have any occupational prejudice against them. I just hate all lawyers regardless of race, creed, color, nationality, or religion. I hate lawyers by definition.

"But Smith, you have lawyers in your own family," someone says, "nephews, shirt tail relatives, even a blood brother, besides several brothers in the faith."

Wrong! Wrong! Wrong!

Please be sure to call my relatives "attorneys," or, if you prefer, call them "legal counselors" or "assistants, as administrative assistants possibly."

The proper definition of lawyer is an admitted member of the bar. This act and deed puts him and other lawyers into a superior status of citizenship. Again, use the term "attorney" or "counselor", please, when referring to someone you respect who practices law putting justice ahead of self.

Each new law or regulation passed in Washington or Austin from unchallenged pettifogging politicians and predator lawyers constitutes another hostage taken from the cause of Freedom and given to tyranny. For 150 years this fair free country enjoyed freedom, with government involvement kept near or below ten percent of the Gross National Product.

I say that each dollar above ten percent, adding any forms of government, forcibly extracted through taxes from the GNP, are dollars of tyranny, tribute paid to lawyers or politicians of like ilk.

Saddam Hussein happens to be among the near recent generation of world dictators and perpetrators of genocide. Though Saddam Hussein put on something of a show during his trial, acting as the judge, director, and leading actor, it resulted in his conviction and death. We still need to be ready for successive perpetrators of genocide, and aggressively turn back runaway government.

I thank God that pursuant to events of 9/11 we had a President who responded with courage, clarity and action to turn this thing around. In contrast to the world scenario of the 1930s, President Bush has kept the course for America with steadfastness and integrity, for which I profoundly thank him.

When you consider presidents or leaders of the past who followed in George Washington's footsteps, it's hard to find many who have given up their offices willingly. Franklin Roosevelt, enthralled with emergency powers, readily used those powers until he died in office during his fourth term. His legacy was runaway government, swollen, and out of control. Twice he defeated his Republican opponents who campaigned with the motto, "No Third Term," which I submit is a tradition worthy of evaluation for not only presidential contests nationally but for all other political offices as well, <u>ALL OF THEM</u>!

Nearly every person at any level in government considers his area of focus important and essential, if not imperative. Have you ever known a person in government, especially a bureaucrat, who has turned back even a portion of "his" appropriation or been willing to reduce his sector of government budget for the next fiscal year or period?

I haven't.

Like Saddam Hussein, pettifogging politicians, predator lawyers, and bureaucrats such as my next door neighbor, County Tax Assessor and Collector, Carl Smith (no kin), enjoy and almost all live to wield power. For years I knew a state politician who was re-elected six times and who was manifestly honest, winsome and friendly. He was absolutely certain of three things: (1) What he did for his "constituents" was only for their good; (2) He was the best qualified person for his job; and (3) Like FDR, he felt there should be no limits as to how long he could remain in office.

My friend also ultimately died in office.

The tendency to control runs in almost all of us.

We were born to be free, and at both the founding of our United States and the founding of Texas, this was understood. But since 1930 we've done a mighty poor job with our freedom. The critical mass of viable freedom diminishes rapidly.

With the tendency to control a part of our biochemical

individuality, also to make more laws, we steal from others by force of taxes, showing the same stuff manifest by every pettifogging politician and predator lawyer anywhere. We tend to want to control. In candor, I'm not exempt from some of those tendencies. Are you?

I submit that there's some lawyer, indeed a little Saddam Hussein, in every darn one

of us.

With the launching of our Constitution and Bill of Rights at a time of great encouragement and hope, someone casually inquired of Benjamin Franklin, "Dr. Franklin, what do we have here?"

He paused, and then answered, "A democracy. If we can keep it."

Ask yourself, can we, are we keeping it?

I submit that the answer is an emphatic <u>no</u>!

It's expedient that I stop here.

This summer Charis and I enjoyed a week-long boat trip down the Danube River of Central Europe, climaxed the final Saturday by an optional World War II visit to Nazi Headquarters at Nuremburg, Germany.

Clearly, manifestly today's German nationals would prefer that citizens visiting their country would "forgive and forget" that tragic, perverse, bizarre, entirely and thoroughly evil chapter of recent German history and all events connected with Adolph Hitler.

Speaking for myself as both a Texan and a United States citizen, I cannot and will not "forgive or forget."

32. Economics Anyone?

What's your opinion of economics?

Did you study it in high school or college?

My dictionary defines economics as "the science of production, distribution and consumption of goods and services." That's a very broad subject, about as broad as the horizon, enough to daunt most anyone, unless for whatever reasons you have chosen to remove yourself from these pivotal concerns.

As you probably know, someone called economics "the dismal science," a label that sticks to this day. That person, I think, was Milton Friedman. Did you find economics dismal?

I did, at least at first.

As a college sophomore, I took an introductory course taught by the Chairman of the Economics Department at UT, Austin, which I expected would be great. Instead it turned out to be a great disappointment.

Let me tell you about that bad experience which I call Economics 101; translate, "Academic" Economics. Sitting in a large classroom, eager to learn, notebook and pencil at the ready, I listened to a man I couldn't understand who lectured voluminously, continuously, and curiously. Though Dr. Steen was angry, he spoke in well framed sentences that added up to nothing. Sometimes he would click his heals nervously as he paced in front of the large window that was usually open to the sidewalk outside.

One day our fraternity dog Rhodes vaulted through a similar window in nearby Seton Hall, breaking up the class with laughter. I always hoped that might happen in Dr. Steen's Economics class, but alas I had to listen to his drivel.

To me Dr. Steen's economics just did not connect. It was indeed dismal. I did not understand him. As the date for our first six weeks' exam approached, I only had a half page of notes, mostly his Social Science buzz words: mores, folkways, cultural norms, etc. The night before the exam I dropped in on a classmate, Jack Pew, a smart quiet guy from Dallas.

"Jack," I said, "you've got to help me. I'm embarrassed to say that I have no idea what this economics professor Dr. Steen is talking about."

"Davo, I don't have any idea what he's talking about either," Jack replied to my surprise. Since neither one of us understood what he was talking about, we pulled together our scant notes and discussed strategy before we decided to "wing it." Since it was to be an essay type exam, we settled on tossing back to Dr. Steen our prolific, esoteric elaboration on his Social Science buzz words. We would just write, write, write, write, and keep writing till either the bell rang or Dr. Steen stopped us.

Next week we learned our strategy worked! Jack had made an "A" and I made a "B!"

So I told Jack, "With these grades I'm sure of three things: I don't know what Dr. Steen is talking about; you don't know what Dr. Steen is talking about; and, Dr. Steen doesn't know what he's talking about either!"

But forget Economics 101, if you too have had a bad

experience with "academic" economics. Fortunately and gratefully I got a second shot at this important subject when I learned of a marvelous outfit called Foundation for Economic Education. One of its founders was a columnist for *Newsweek* magazine, Henry Hazlitt, who wrote a book with the ambitious title *Economics In One Lesson*, which I have come to call Economics 102. Hazlitt's "Economics..." was neither dismal nor daunting but clear, trenchant and incisive.

Let me give you Henry Hazlitt's *Economics In One Lesson* reduced by him to this single sentence:

THE ART OF ECONOMICS CONSISTS IN LOOKING NOT MERELY AT THE IMMEDIATE BUT AT THE LONGER EFFECTS OF ANY ACT OR POLICY; IT CONSISTS IN TRACING THE CONSEQUENCES OF THAT POLICY, NOT MERELY FOR ONE GROUP BUT FOR ALL GROUPS.

One day I plan to open a bookstore and will feature Hazlitt's *Economics in One Lesson* at five to eight dollars a copy. In his foreword to the book, Steve Forbes describes it as "a book so powerful in clarity and simplicity that we can declare, without question, that it has shaped our world." It is also endorsed by Nobel Laureates in Economics Milton Friedman and F. A. Hayek.

This seminal book has sold over a million copies and been translated into numerous languages. It should be <u>required</u> reading for all public servants and all pettifogging politicians, <u>before they run for office</u>.

The book's importance lies in what might happen if enough citizens take its implications seriously. As still free citizens, we might, emphasis **might**, regain control of this runaway government that not only takes from us but also spends near half of our gross national product. We should be outraged! Unless we promptly, systematically, and substantially reduce government in this generation, we shall lose our freedom sooner than we know.

Marvelous! Hear, Hear! Amen! for Economics 102 by Henry Hazlitt.

After college and army days when I was struggling with my chemical business, my interest in economics was piqued and challenged by a PhD economist at SMU, Paul T. Heyne. Dr. Heyne had written a marvelous introductory economics text that was anything but dismal, with large amusing photographs, wide margins, easy to read print and interesting issues.

In Dallas I looked up Dr. Heyne to express my appreciation for his textbook, entitled *The Economic Way of Thinking*, which I call Economics 103. Dr. Heyne told me that though his book was a success, a second edition was at the printers even then because he had so much neat, good new stuff to share with students. I am eternally grateful for Dr. Heyne and his classic textbook, Economics 103, which went through at least nine editions over his lifetime. A group of Heyne's protégés at the University of Seattle brought out the 10th edition after he passed away.

At one time Galena Park School District did not teach Economics 103, which gave me an idea! I would offer each high school graduate a copy of Heyne's book if the graduate promised to read it. So I called Heyne's publisher at SRI, knowing that the second edition of Dr. Heyne's *Economic Way of Thinking* was soon to be released. I asked the sales representative, "Sir, what would be the price to me if I were to buy up the remainder of Dr. Heyne's first edition?"

The salesman perked up, told me how great the book was, and after running through a calculation, quoted me a modest discount from his regular price.

"Sir, have you read Dr. Heyne's economic text yourself?" I asked. He claimed that he had.

"Well then, may I suggest you read chapter six again before you turn down my low offer which I'm sending you by mail." The lesson in chapter six was: sunk costs are really sunk! My offer to the salesman was one dollar a copy for some couple hundred copies. When he called me back, he did so with a laugh, but accepted my offer. Heyne's chapter six did the trick in one important lesson, "Sunk costs are really sunk."

Haply and happily a good number of Galena Park High School graduates received a copy of Heyne's *Economic Way of Thinking*, which I call "Economics 103," as a graduation present.

Heyne's *Private Keepers of the Public Interest* is a superb title for the reason that it talks about freedom. *Private Keepers* – of the *public interest;* don't miss that! It refers to you and me and hundreds of fellow citizens who enjoy the fruits of our own labor, who work for a living at an occupation of our choice to the extent that the free market will pay us. Private Keepers, NOT pettifogging politicians are the epitome of Hayne's economics as advocated by both Hazlitt and Hayne.

How I hope and pray that we can turn around this ruinous runaway government that is eroding our still free economy law by law, dollar by dollar, moving us toward a compromised economy.

So here are three kinds of Economics as I see them.

- Economics 101 – "academic" economics which tends to be dull and dismal
- Economics 102 – Hazlitt's *Economics in One Lesson* and/or
- Economics 103 – Heyne's *Private Keepers of the Public Interest*, all three are great, alive, relevant, even fascinating.

What about Economics 104? This, my friend, you will learn from life itself as you offer your skills and services in our still free economy, in the work place. Perhaps you will enhance these applied economics with experience and informal education, but more importantly while working, giving and venturing in our still free economy.

33. Financial Whorehouses All Over Texas

What Texans think long about, we are apt to think rightly about. A few years back the *Houston Chronicle* published several lengthy articles concerning the low morale of employees at the Lottery Commission, which was said to be down. In one of the stories the lead lines were: "Lottery at Will Firings Keep Employees on Edge. Lawmakers and Workers Decry an Atmosphere of Fear, Mistrust at the Commission."

Ha!

How interesting, ironic, and compassionately perverse that the *Chronicle* should be to concern itself with fears and poor morale of employees at the Lottery Commission.

Morale problems are minuscule alongside the social problems the lottery creates in the areas of crime, addiction, and bankruptcy. These are three major impacts on victims of gambling, the politicians welcomed into our State with the lottery by the *Chronicle*.

Has the *Chronicle* ever considered the "morale" and atmosphere of "fear" of fellow Texans who with increasing numbers fall prey to the false promise of hope and dreams dangled in front of them by the Lottery Commission?

We have the legislators in Austin and also the apathy of Texas voters to thank for letting this mad bitch get over the wall into our otherwise prosperous state.

From 1992 until 2005 the Texas Lottery aggressively

maintained that the players of the lottery made between "$40k and $60k a year, were college educated, and white." This "Big Lie" did not stop until a 2005 demographic study conducted by the Earl Survey Research Laboratory at Texas Tech University revealed what has been obvious to growing numbers in Texas since the beginning. It was Texans and minorities *with low income* and *lower education* levels who were playing the lottery. A great number are addicted to lottery gambling, which at this writing is promoted by some 18,000 Financial Whorehouses, everywhere easily available in Texas

The Texas Tech study is not the sole proof that mostly the poor are playing the lottery. LG Inc. is a consulting and research outfit in Austin that provides expertise and empirical data that also reveal the economic and demographic breakdown of the Texas Lottery players. Lottery Group is a company headed by Mr. Rob Kohler, who spent twelve years at the Lottery Commission prior to starting his company. By looking at actual lottery sales broken down by legislative districts and the 2000 census data for these districts, LG's thorough analysis leaves no doubt about who the lottery players are. Let us share with others some demographic and fiscal year 2005 lottery sales in the Greater Houston Area provided by Lottery Group. First, let's look at annual per capita income.

[Insert "Annual Per Capita Income" graph]

The annual per capita income in Houston is as low as $10,000 in Rep. Bailey's district, and as high as $51,000 in Rep. Wong's district. I point out that proponents for the lottery in Texas argue that players are only using disposable income to play the lottery. Not so. It comes right out of families/persons low income needed for basics: food, clothing, housing, medical care, etc.

When you divide $10,000 in annual income by 12 months, it's easy to see that there is no disposable income in a monthly salary of $833. In fact, most of these Texas families are not only living in sub-standard conditions without health or car insurance but are likely receiving some form of public dole as well.

Next look at the educational attainment levels in these same districts:

The percentage of individuals 25 years and older who have earned bachelors degrees or higher in Houston is as low as 3.6% in Rep. Bailey's district, and as high was 66.6% in Rep. Wong's district. The districts with the lower incomes have corresponding low levels of education. There is an education crisis in Texas, but concentrate for the moment this quarter and this year on driving this despicable curse of pettifogging politicians and predator lawyers out of Texas with deliberate speed.

(Take a look at selected labor and income characteristics in these same districts.)

The percentage of population living in poverty in Houston is as high as 25.9% in Rep. Dutton's district, and as low as 4.1% in Rep. Howard's district.

The percentage of household incomes that include public assistance in Houston is as high as 5.6% in Rep. Dutton's district, and as low as .5% in Rep. Wong's district.

The percentage of total unemployment in Houston is as high as 13.1% in Rep. Coleman's district, and as low as 3.1% in Rep. Wong's district, a fourfold difference.

Let's look at Black and Hispanic voting age population

in these same districts.

The percentage of Black and Hispanic population living in Houston is as high as 78.8% in Rep. Dutton's district, and as low as 13.8% in Rep. Wong's district.

Nearly three quarters of those respondents indicated they earned less than $15,000 per year, and almost half have no health insurance.

Unemployment was and still is a major issue for Katrina evacuees. <u>Less than 20%</u> of the respondents to the survey are employed.

Houston only scratched the surface on understanding the full effects of Katrina. Without a doubt the economics and demographics of our city have and will continue to change.

But let's take a look at the graph of Texas' fiscal year 2005 lottery sales by district.

While the Texas Lottery would have its citizens believe that the lottery sales are coming out of Rep. Wong's most college educated and white district, please note that the FY 2005 lottery sales in Houston were as high as $48.8 million in Rep. Coleman's district, and as low as $17.2 million in Rep. Callegari's district. Rep. Wong's district had sales of $19.7 million.

Rep. Coleman's district had over twice the lottery sales of Rep. Wong's district. Can this be true? Let's look at the demographic data of these two districts again:

That's right, gambling of all kinds, and no less the lottery, preys decidedly on minorities and the poor. Without a doubt the "Big Lie" is revealed. <u>The fact that Rep. Coleman's district has the highest unemployment in Houston as well as the highest lottery sales should be</u>

enough reason for our promoting dismemberment of the Lottery Commission.

Has anyone counted the ultimate cost in welfare taxes for the desperate person, hooked to addiction, who fantasizes he can gamble his way out of compounding debt via the lottery?

Careful research by varied responsible institutions such as the University of Illinois put the range of so-called recreational gamblers who become compulsive gamblers at from three to eight percent!

The Texas Lottery's own demographic studies substantiate the fact that Texans who can least afford it play the lottery the most. In the December 2005 study conducted by the Earl Survey Research Laboratory at Texas Tech University, the summary reports that "White lottery players report spending less per month on lottery games than non-white lottery players." The study also reports that players with less than a high school education spent $173.17 a month on the lottery, compared to $48.61 for players with college degrees.

Additionally, the study reports that White players spent $55.02 a month, compared to $108.96 for Black players, and $102.20 for Hispanic players.

In anticipating any counter arguments to this data, it is important to look at a "macro" view of the lottery activities in Houston. The next graph covers at the last three years of lottery sales by district.

The chart clearly demonstrates a predatory trend of lottery sales in Houston. The State of Texas' financial prostitution of the citizens in Rep. Coleman's district and districts like his should be unacceptable to all Texans when exposed to this data. Like exhausting the pools of oil in any given oil field, the State of Texas is exploiting and will eventually exhaust one of its most precious resources, the capital and potential of its citizens, particularly the poorest and least educated. It is a sad and sick day when the lottery is being glorified and advertised throughout Texas. The Lottery Commission's leadership even has the audacity to compare the lottery to parents going door to door selling cookies for our schools. It is criminal that Texas' funds are being used to promulgate this "Big Lie", and cynical that *these funds have come from Texans who can least afford it.*

Many of the people who "indulge" in this "cheap, harmless fun" fail to consider the secondary consequences as well as the long-term effects of what they are doing.

Let's carry the analogy of financial prostitution further. With some 16,000 locations throughout Texas, there is sure to be a State Lottery "financial whorehouse" in a strip center near you with a lottery pimp or madam ready to take your money.

The "whorehouse" itself may not be as glitzy as the ones across in Louisiana, and decked out for you to "scratch off" but the slick tickets themselves and the gaudy dispensers surely are.

Have you every stood in line at the HEB and watched some poor soul puzzle over which scratch ticket to buy? Exasperating, isn't it? And it's also sad. Sometimes it would seem the fellow is praying.

What's amazing is that retailers selling lottery tickets in Texas have made public their reasons for selling the tickets. Is it because they make money off the tickets? No.... Is it

because they like the idea of selling the tickets? No....
Retailers find that they make no money on selling lottery
tickets. They have to offer lottery tickets because the store
across the street is offering them. The product is a loser. In
fact, retailers in Texas receive only five cents on every
dollar spent on a lottery ticket, and they receive no
compensation for the use of their operating capital to pay
prizes. When compared to the earnings of retailers in other
states that offer the same services for their states' lotteries,
Texas retailers come out on the bottom.

We Texans may often be slow learners; however,
ultimately we do learn. . . . maybe!

When do you think retailers will do the arithmetic and
figure out how much business they're losing from the
money sinkhole? Which store or food chains will be the
first to wake up and have the guts to turn down their
pitiful lottery revenue and the net financial damage to
Texas' poorest and least education citizens, especially
Blacks and Hispanics? HEB, maybe?

I must point out that the Texas Lottery recently took
steps to increase the financial incentive for retailers selling
their product, be it unknowingly and with long-term
negative financial implications for all Texans. Beginning in
1992 through 2003 the Texas Lottery introduced around 30
instant games a year, at scratch ticket prices of $1, $2 and
$5. Over 120 games were released in 2005, running the cost
of a scratch ticket up to $20, $25 and $30. Retailers have
gone from being compensated five cents for a one dollar
scratch ticket to receiving $1.50 for selling a $30 scratch
ticket. Good for retailers, bad for the poor souls who are
putting $30 down on an impulse buy that is designed for

<u>them to lose</u>.

I say scratching off a lottery game ticket is like scratching under your own skin with a dirty needle that's been used by a person infected with AIDS, FINANCIAL AIDS. It is difficult to envision what sort of cheap, vacuous thrill some persons derive from this but it is surely there.

The economic impact and out-of-pocket rip-offs on Texas are huge; specifically the $42 billion dollars that have been wagered on the Texas Lottery since its inception. That much misspent and totally wasted money might otherwise have been used to pay the rent, buy shoes, and groceries, or could have been invested in savings accounts, homes, a 401(k) plan or other worthy investments. That's the negative impact on the Texas economy from the Texas Lottery's "little harmless fun" for probably someone you know, maybe even friends or relatives.

<u>What would happen</u> if Texans invested the <u>$42 billion dollars</u> in small legitimate businesses over the State? Basically we have an excellent place for business in Texas, with more <u>business owners than union members</u>. Jobs come from small businesses. They do not come from the Department of Labor or from the Lottery Commission, nor from the President of the United States either directly or indirectly, neither from the past Texas governor, nor the next possible candidate if he/she favors the lottery.

Do you have an idea for a new business? Encourage friends to start putting the money they spend on the lottery into your business. That's got to be a far better bet than lottery tickets, which are <u>based on fraud, weakness, and dishonesty</u>.

Do you realize that you and I tacitly approve the

government's theft from fellow Texas citizens through its waste of $42 billion by the Lottery Commission? This is where financial prostitution becomes financial AIDS. And there are no psychological condoms to prevent financial AIDS, not from Medicare or from the psychological drug store.

Or, look at it this way. The lottery is a cancer that is eating up our society. It may be that neither I nor others want Texans playing the lottery, but that does not free us from dealing with the costs and damage caused by its existence. My family and I share the same hospitals and healthcare facilities as those individuals who are spending their last pennies on false dreams promoted through the lottery. I pay increased health insurance premiums and fees at these facilities to compensate for patients who are unable to pay their own health care costs. We share the same police and county services. Charis and I pay for increased crime, addiction, bankruptcies and despair through local and state taxes, directly and indirectly through the Texas Lottery.

Enough is enough! We do not live in a fish bowl. Even though we do not play the lottery, we are paying for the fraud against other Texans, especially the most vulnerable of our society.

You and I need to hold the pettifogging politicians / predator lawyers responsible for this ugly, asinine, colossal rip-off that is the lottery. We must stay after the Austin crowd till we get the whole disgusting string of financial whorehouses out of our great State of Texas.

The most important step is to drive out the pettifogging politicians/predator lawyers who continue to allow wanton fraudulent financial whorehouses (some 8,000 of them) to operate throughout the State of Texas.

Rep. Martha Wong and Senator Mario Gallegos are my representatives in Austin that I plan to personally see about this miserable lottery.

Who are yours? Do the same, will you please?

Let's take action to drive the lottery out of Texas with deliberate speed.

34. Stop Runaway Government

STOP!
STOP it, I say.
Stop runaway government.
Don't kill it, just stop it.

In the 1990s I sketched away at some essays on things important to me, mostly fun things about places like "Live Oak Ranch" and "Jogging Around Rice," not thinking I could change the world before breakfast tomorrow morning, nor even by the next election.

These days I'm neither a Republican nor a Democrat, with friends, employees, and fellow church members on both sides of the aisle.

No one can deny his own experience and mine has been one of profound thankfulness for this free land that is ours where all of us have the right to be heard, to express our opinions, to start a new business without having to ask or kneel or beg from some high priest of government in Washington or Austin. Freedoms of most kinds we still have in most areas.

Entitlements are another matter. Whoever cooked up that sorry word should be shot!

Not really. You know I didn't mean it, but you also need to know I'm against the mistaken notion that we are entitled to much of anything just because of who we are or are not, whether to be wasps, or gringos, or lily livered loons, or "whatever".

WASPS? Maybe? Maybe be a wasp or hornet of some kind or another. Have you every been stung by a bee? Emphatically not pleasant.

HORNETS? That's all right emotionally, but way down the line in the peck order from being a tiger at El Paso High School (good) or a panther at Austin High School (bad). Tea Sips are to tigers what Aggies are to panthers. Does that make any sense in your Texas baby book?

We do have rights and freedoms, many in fact nearly most of the freedoms set forth by our founding fathers in our Constitution and Bill of Rights though at least here in Texas some are under attack, perhaps eroding fast.

Freedom is first and foremost.

What's your view on freedom, especially to start up a new business?

How long has it been since you started up a business?

First we should ask if any of you have started up a new business.

At least some of the persons reading this . . . _____?

I hope not _____.

Office of The Handicapper General
OOHG USA

But entitlements? No way! Right to life?
Maybe.

35. Where Do Jobs Come From?

(Optimal Employment)

It is amazing what numerous and sometimes strange notions people have as to where jobs come from. As a person who puts economics second in importance to sound education, I ask you rhetorically to express yourself in answering the question, "Where <u>do</u> jobs come from?"

Variations on these themes cover a few important but mistaken notions harbored by many fellow citizens.

A good many times a person has come to me over the years in seriousness asking, "Will you gimme a job?"

Apparently those persons will add the adjective, "stingy employers," supposing that all one has to do is for the employer to answer "yes." It is in fact essential for you to add that you are going to at least consider a counter question, "How are you qualified for this or any other job?"

That still begs the question of how jobs originate in the first place.

"From the Government."

Petty fogging politicians and predator lawyers love to think that they have a great deal to do with generating jobs.

Full employment is something all of us hope for and in most cases work toward.

When I was a little boy growing up in Far West Texas at the bottom of The Great Depression, I vividly remember tramps riding on railroad freight cars, beggars politely calling at our house on Mississippi Street asking for a bite of breakfast, and my giving it to them – cinnamon rolls.

At Dudley School boys and girls played separately for the most part, and talked separately most of the time.

As teenagers Dad Smith emphatically taught each of his three boys that there were three things you didn't discuss.

1. Politics. The reason? For some reason, it had a way of unmaking friends.
2. Religion. It raised more questions than it answered and promoted more discord than harmony.
3. Sex. No reason given.

But there was one matter our father taught us that every father should teach his sons and daughters as well: how to work.

Both Dad and Uncle Hope taught me how to work, agencies of FDR's government notwithstanding to the contrary; albeit before the days of NKVD.

The summer we turned 13 each of us had to go out and find himself a job. We did it on our own, alone except for public transportation.

From Dad and Uncle Hope I also learned two things of pivotal importance concerning work:

Except for part-time, do NOT work for your
family company or in-laws.

The spectra of favoritism always hangs over what you do or don't do, inadequate blame when things go wrong, too little compensation or credit when you do well.

For five summers I worked for Uncle Hope at Magnolia Coca-Cola Bottling Co., and each summer I became a bit more convinced that this might not be what I should do as my life's work.

A couple of events were defining; first, as route drivers arrived in late summer afternoons, we all worked together putting off dealing with the two dozen brute wooden crates, until all truck drivers had checked in together with the day's cash receipts. That was before the days of forklift operators.

I was a helper, which meant I got to do the heavy, grunt work, hefting at least five crates to a hand truck, often 20 or 30 stairs below street level.

A Chinese restaurant owner on South El Paso street delighted in making me negotiate a couple dozen wooden stairs maybe five inches wide and seven tall down to his dark basement where I would unload my full cases, pick up the empties and negotiate my way back up to street level.

Good exercise for all fractures or hernia training, though I wasn't a jock.

Most drivers and helpers at Magnolia Coca-Cola wore their white uniforms with the large red coke emblem called bull's eyes on their back with pride.

When the truck drivers arrived back at the plant after a long day's work, all drivers and helpers (loaders) alike pitched in, working together till all trucks were unloaded of empties, then reloaded with fulls (each weighing about 40 pounds) to go out first thing the next morning.

Delicious and Refreshing